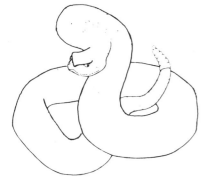

Reptiles and Amphibians

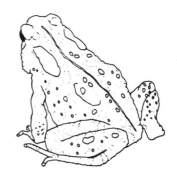

Sarah Anne Hughes

Roger Tory Peterson,
Robert C. Stebbins, and Roger Conant,
Consulting Editors

Sponsored by the
National Wildlife Federation
and the Roger Tory Peterson Institute

Houghton Mifflin Company Boston New York

To Clare Cuddy and Dean Klaudt,
in gratitude for their
friendship and support.

Copyright © 1985 by
Houghton Mifflin Company

Visit our Web site:
www.houghtonmifflinbooks.com.

ISBN 0-618-30737-0 (pbk.)

Printed in the
United States of Ameica

DPI 10 9 8 7 6 5 4 3 2 1

Introduction

Finding reptiles and amphibians is a visual activity; it trains the eye. Most nature-oriented people who become interested in snakes, lizards, turtles, frogs, and salamanders soon acquire *A Field Guide to Reptiles and Amphibians of Eastern and Central North America* or its western counterpart, *A Field Guide to Western Reptiles and Amphibians*. These guides offer short cuts to recognition, using little arrows that point to the special features by which one creature may be known from a similar one. The herpetologists, as the afficionados of this branch of natural history are called, have a distinct advantage. Unlike most birdwatchers, they can catch and handle their animals, and unlike botanists and entomologists, who must dry and mount their specimens if they wish to preserve them, they can keep their captives alive — even enjoy them as pets.

This coloring book will sharpen your observations and condition your memory for the days you spend out-of-doors. By filling in the colors during evenings at home or on winter days before spring brings the world to life, you will be better informed about these fascinating, creepy, crawly things when you chance to find them.

A coloring book such as this will help your color perception, but it will not teach you to draw, unless you copy the basic line drawings so artfully prepared by Sarah Hughes. You might even try to sketch turtles or frogs in the field, if only roughly in pencil. Snakes are not so easy.

Exploring the outdoors, searching for reptiles and amphibians can be many things — an art, a science, a game, or a sport — but above all it sharpens the senses, especially the eye. If you draw or paint, the sense of touch also comes into play; the images of the eye and the mind are transferred by hand to paper. In the process, you become more aware of the natural world — the real world — and inevitably you become an environmentalist.

Most of you will find colored pencils best suited for coloring this book, but if you are handy with brushes and paints, you may prefer to fill in the outlines with watercolors. Crayons, too, can be used. But don't labor; have fun.

Roger Tory Peterson

About This Book

You may already be familiar with many of the animals in this book — perhaps you have found a toad in the yard or seen a turtle in a nearby pond. But many of the species will be new to you. Coloring the pictures in this book will help you learn to identify them.

However, animals are not identified only by their colors. Shape, size, behavior, and occasionally very small details such as scales also distinguish the different species. Two other books will help you learn to recognize these animals: *A Field Guide to Reptiles and Amphibians of Eastern and Central North America* by Roger Conant and Joseph Collins and *A Field Guide to Western Reptiles and Amphibians* by Robert C. Stebbins. These books will also give you more information about where to look for reptiles and amphibians.

Not all the animals shown in this book will occur in your area. But you can enjoy learning about reptiles and amphibians from other parts of the country, perhaps to prepare for a vacation or as a winter's activity when many of these animals hibernate to escape the cold.

How to Use This Book

You can use crayons, watercolors, or colored pencils to color the drawings. The colors of individual reptiles and amphibians vary. Don't be too concerned about matching the colors on the stickers exactly, as they are just a guide.

Try mixing your colors on the page. For example, you can create olive-brown by blending two or three crayon colors. A frog that is olive-brown will be more green in some parts, and more brown in others — it will not be a solid, even color all over. This variation gives these animals their vibrant colors. Even drab browns and greens have life in them.

Animals with moist skins, such as amphibians, show highlights. These areas on their bodies reflect light and are usually left white in a drawing. Adding highlights to the drawings will make them look more alive. Also, don't forget the shadows. Darker areas will show under the head, body, limbs, and tail. You might want to add a shadow to the page, where the animal is blocking the light. A solid, dark shadow with a clear edge indicates strong sunlight, and this would be appropriate for desert reptiles. A diffuse shadow suggests gentle sunlight. Above all, have fun with your coloring.

Amphibians. The first group of animals in this book includes the salamanders, frogs, and toads. These are all amphibians. They have damp, scaleless skins and, although they move about on land, always need moist surroundings. While many have lungs and gills as larvae (young), they also "breathe" through their skins, which must remain moist to absorb oxygen. They are "cold-blooded" animals. This means they cannot warm themselves with muscular movements such as shivering, as mammals are able to do, nor can they sweat to cool off. Since many don't move very rapidly, they are usually easy to watch. The trick is to find them, because they are often well camouflaged and frequently hide during the day under logs and in damp holes.

Adult salamanders, frogs, and toads return to the water to breed and lay eggs. In most species, the larvae remain in the water until they become adults. They are all carnivorous as adults, eating insects and other live prey.

Reptiles. Crocodiles, turtles, lizards, and snakes are all reptiles. Their scaly skin allows them to live on land, since it protects them from drying out. Some reptiles, such as turtles, have special adaptations for living in water, including limbs that have developed into flippers. However, all reptiles, even water-adapted turtles, return to land to lay their eggs. These leathery or hard-shelled eggs are laid in soil or loose sand and left to develop on their own. When hatched, the

The parts of a turtle's shell

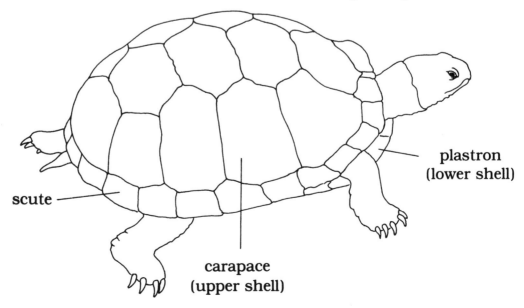

scute

plastron (lower shell)

carapace (upper shell)

young dig themselves out and usually fend for themselves without help from their parents.

Like amphibians, reptiles are "cold-blooded." But they can control their temperature by their behavior. Basking in the sun on a warm rock, on a log, or in shallow water raises their body temperature to a point where they can be active. In hot environments like the desert, they avoid the extreme heat of the day and move about only at night or in the early morning and late afternoon or evening.

Finding Reptiles and Amphibians. Many reptiles and amphibians move rapidly or hide quickly, and you rarely have time to study them before they disappear. It helps to learn their habits before you go out into the field, and also to know a little about what you might find. For example, animals live in specific habitats. You need not look for a Desert Tortoise in the Pacific Northwest forests; it lives in the deserts of the Southwest. In a Pacific Northwest forest, look for frogs and salamanders.

One good way to learn about the reptiles and amphibians in your area is to choose a wild area — a place where animals live undisturbed, such as a pond, marsh, or woodland — and visit it regularly. Get to know it well. Visit at various times of the year and at different times of the day. Don't forget that many animals are active when we are usually asleep. You will become familiar with the animals that live there. At first, you may catch just a glimpse of a snake or turtle, but the next time at the same place you will be ready. Perhaps you will even be there first, waiting when "your" turtle arrives at the water's edge.

Whenever you look for animals, remember that they can be frightened by sudden movements and noise or vibrations. While it's fun to take a dog for a walk, leave it behind if you want to see reptiles and amphibians. The dog's activity will frighten them into their hiding places long before you can spot them. A good way to observe animals is to choose a sunny, quiet place and sit still, waiting for animals to come near. By being there first, you may be able to watch them for some time and see their markings more clearly.

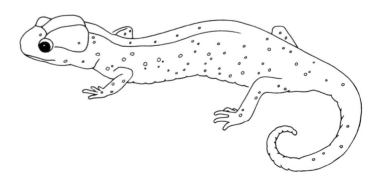

Species Differences. The reptiles and amphibians that you see in the field may not look exactly like the ones in this book. Each animal is an individual and may differ from the general pattern for the species. Some reptiles and amphibians vary substantially from this general pattern and form distinct populations which are called subspecies. Subspecies are closely related to each other; some look almost identical, but others look different enough to be given a separate name. Several of the animals shown in this book are subspecies, and the ones in your area may not look like the drawings. Try making sketches or notes on these differences, and keep a record of the things that you see in your area. This way you will know how your local reptiles and amphibians differ from the illustrations.

Conserving Reptiles and Amphibians

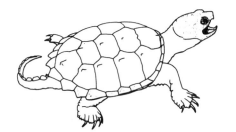

Like all animals, reptiles and amphibians can live only in certain kinds of places. If their homes are destroyed, they may die. Their needs are complex. Many amphibians have lost their habitats through the draining of swamps or pollution of the waters on which they depend. Some are so rare that they are in danger of disappearing forever. You can help by knowing where the reptiles and amphibians live in your area and protecting these places.

Sarah Anne Hughes

Mudpuppy

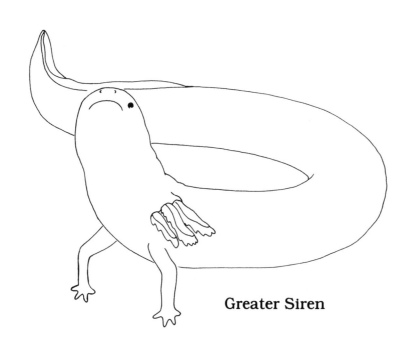

Greater Siren

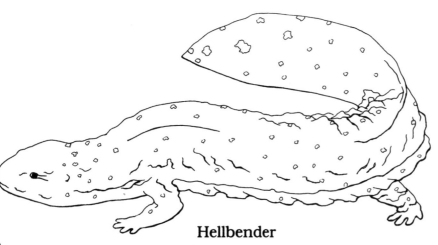

Hellbender

Salamanders

Most salamanders have elongate, moist-skinned bodies and limbs without claws. These amphibians are found in damp habitats. Most live on land for part of the year, returning to the water to breed and lay eggs. The larvae (young) of most species have feathery external gills that disappear as they mature into adults. Some remain in the larval form all their lives, staying in the water and keeping their gills. Take along a glass jar when looking for these animals. They are easily hurt by handling, and can best be watched for a short time in a jar. Return them carefully to the same place where you found them.

Mudpuppy
Since this salamander remains a larva all its life, it never loses its bright maroon or reddish gills. Blue-black spots mark its gray or rusty brown skin. It is active at night in ponds and slowly flowing streams, hunting aquatic prey. (1)

Greater Siren
An eel-like salamander of weedy southern rivers. The forelegs are small and often hidden by the large gills. Its skin is gray to olive, slightly darker on the back than on the sides. (2)

Hellbender
The grotesque appearance of this large salamander is not enhanced by its gray or yellowish skin. Black dots occasionally mark the back and sides. Despite their appearance, these animals of quiet streams are quite harmless. (3)

Marbled Salamander

A widespread species, this chunky salamander could also be called the "banded salamander." The crossbands on its back widen at the sides; they are light gray in the female and white in the male. The rest of the body is black. Eggs are laid in shallow depressions before autumn rains, and hatch when covered with water. (4)

Spotted Salamander

You may find Spotted Salamanders in woodland pools, where they gather after warm spring rains. Their mass migrations are a rare and exciting sight. The spots on the upper surfaces are yellow or orange against black, slate, or bluish black. The belly is a lighter slate gray. (5)

Barred Tiger Salamander

This animal also appears in the Prairie Scene, p. 51. It is a subspecies of the Tiger Salamander. A large, active salamander, the Barred Tiger is often seen at night after heavy rain. It emerges from underground hiding places to breed in the spring. The skin is black or dark brown, and the marks along the sides are bright yellow. The marks on the back are not as clear as those on the sides. (6)

Eastern Tiger Salamander

Another subspecies of the Tiger Salamander. Small, irregular, light markings of olive or yellowish brown contrast with this salamander's dull black or brown body. The belly markings are lighter. When not breeding, it lives under plant debris in woods, often near water. (7)

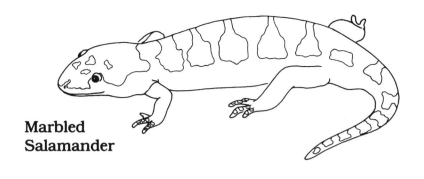
Marbled Salamander

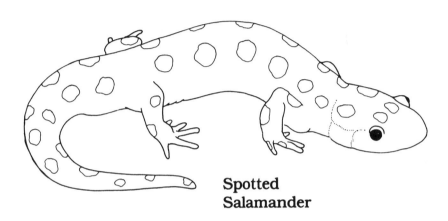
Spotted Salamander

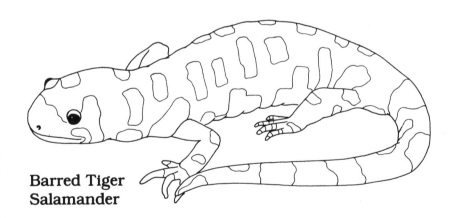
Barred Tiger Salamander

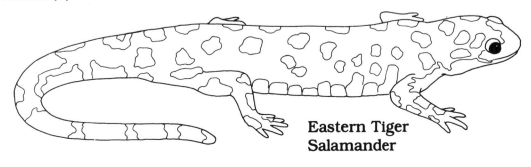
Eastern Tiger Salamander

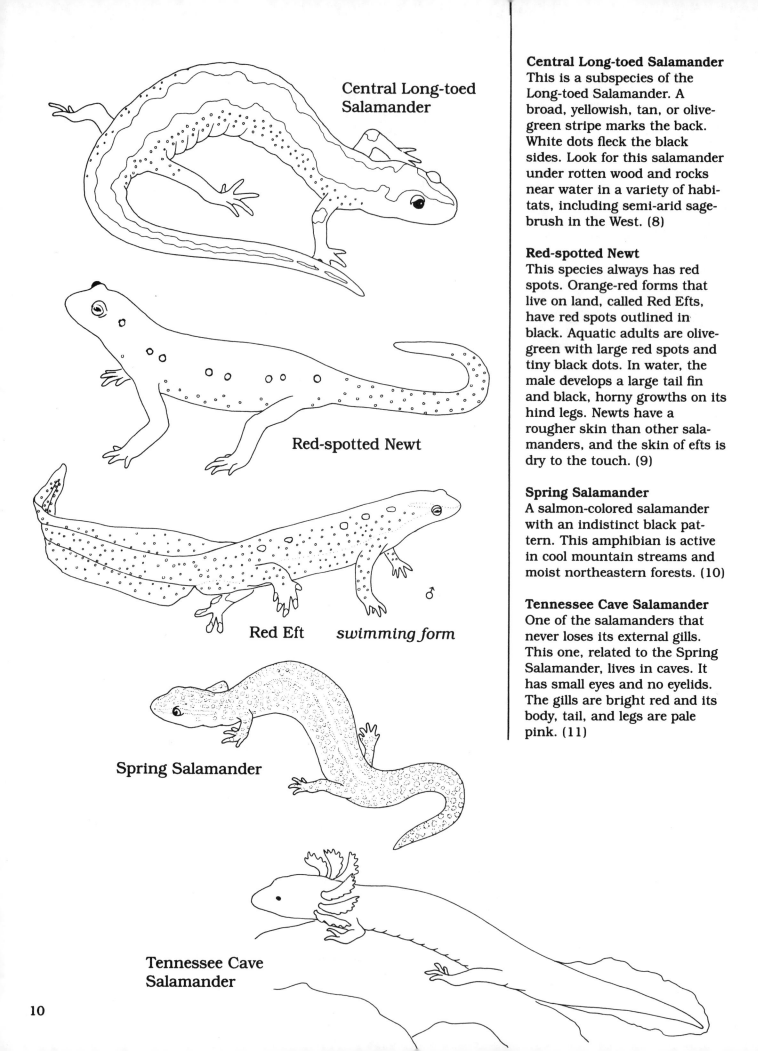

Central Long-toed Salamander

Red-spotted Newt

Red Eft *swimming form* ♂

Spring Salamander

Tennessee Cave Salamander

Central Long-toed Salamander
This is a subspecies of the Long-toed Salamander. A broad, yellowish, tan, or olive-green stripe marks the back. White dots fleck the black sides. Look for this salamander under rotten wood and rocks near water in a variety of habitats, including semi-arid sagebrush in the West. (8)

Red-spotted Newt
This species always has red spots. Orange-red forms that live on land, called Red Efts, have red spots outlined in black. Aquatic adults are olive-green with large red spots and tiny black dots. In water, the male develops a large tail fin and black, horny growths on its hind legs. Newts have a rougher skin than other salamanders, and the skin of efts is dry to the touch. (9)

Spring Salamander
A salmon-colored salamander with an indistinct black pattern. This amphibian is active in cool mountain streams and moist northeastern forests. (10)

Tennessee Cave Salamander
One of the salamanders that never loses its external gills. This one, related to the Spring Salamander, lives in caves. It has small eyes and no eyelids. The gills are bright red and its body, tail, and legs are pale pink. (11)

Western Red-backed Salamander

A salamander of Pacific Northwest forests. The stripe along the back varies in color and extends to the tip of the tail. This stripe may be tan, brown, orange, or yellow. White flecks mark the sides of the body. (12)

Appalachian Woodland Salamander

This salamander appears in such a variety of patterns that many were once named as separate species. Recent research has shown that the patterns blend together and that it is impossible to separate them. Here are four to color. The Metcalf's Salamander is all black or dusky gray. The Clemson Salamander is black with silvery patches and white flecks. The Red-cheeked has a dusky gray body and a red cheek patch, and the Red-legged has red legs. (13)

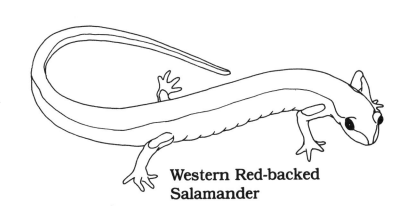

Western Red-backed Salamander

Appalachian Woodland Salamander

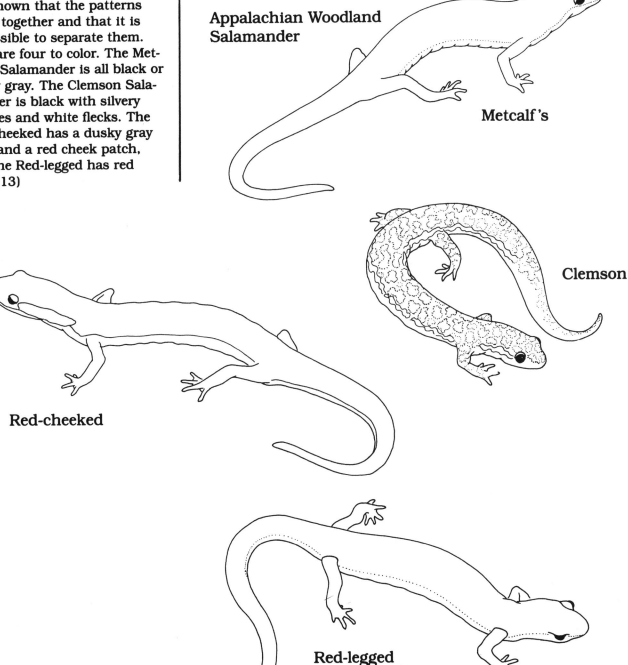

Metcalf's

Clemson

Red-cheeked

Red-legged

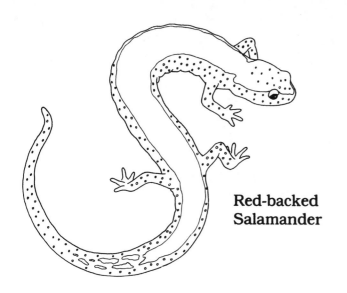

**Red-backed
Salamander**

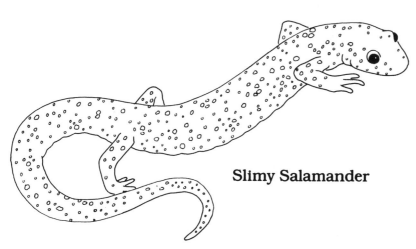

Slimy Salamander

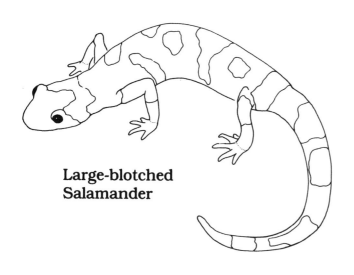

**Large-blotched
Salamander**

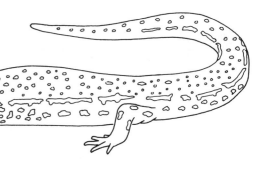

**Northern Dusky
Salamander**

Red-backed Salamander
A commonly encountered salamander in the Northeast
woods. It appears in two forms.
The truly red-backed form has
a broad, straight-edged, red
dorsal stripe. The "lead-backed"
form is uniformly dark gray.
(14)

Slimy Salamander
Slimy, or more correctly, sticky
secretions from its skin protect
this woodland salamander from
predators. The large black body
is flecked with silvery white
spots, sometimes mixed with
brassy colored spots. (15)

Large-blotched Salamander
A black and orange amphibian.
Its bands and limb bases are
orange. This brightly marked
salamander seeks damp places
in western deciduous and ever-
green forests. (16)

Northern Dusky Salamander
A variable salamander. Its body
is usually gray or brown, with
markings just dark enough to
show. This amphibian is sel-
dom found far from running
water. (17)

Northern Red Salamander

A bright red or orange animal with a spattering of black spots on the upper surfaces. Older individuals have a darker body and large spots. (18)

Eastern Mud Salamander

A number of round black spots dot this red salamander. As its name indicates, it likes muddy places near springs and small streams. (19)

Northern Two-lined Salamander

The yellow back is outlined by dark brown stripes. The belly is brighter yellow. This salamander is common along rocky streams in the Northeast. (20)

Cave Salamander

This long-tailed salamander may be yellow, orange, or bright red. The spots are black. The prehensile (grasping) tail helps it climb along slippery rocks at cave entrances. It also may be found in open spaces. (21)

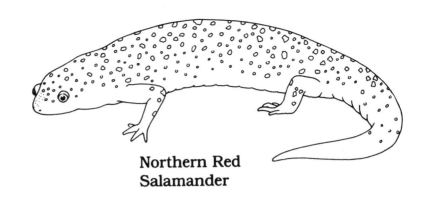

Northern Red
Salamander

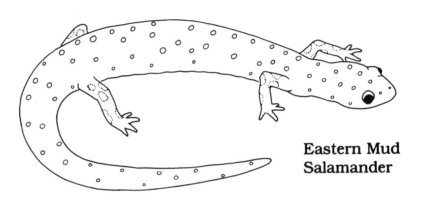

Eastern Mud
Salamander

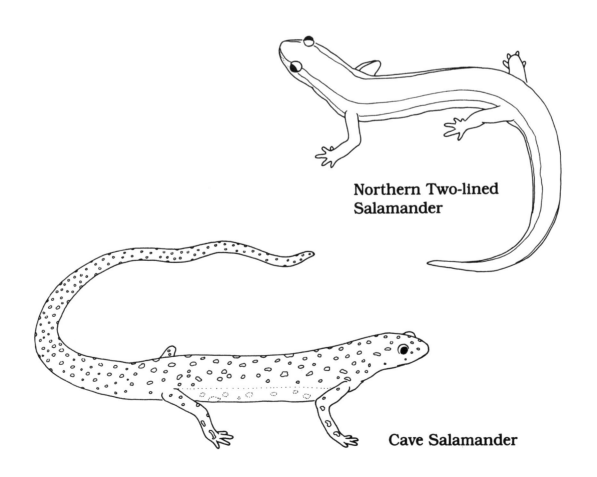

Northern Two-lined
Salamander

Cave Salamander

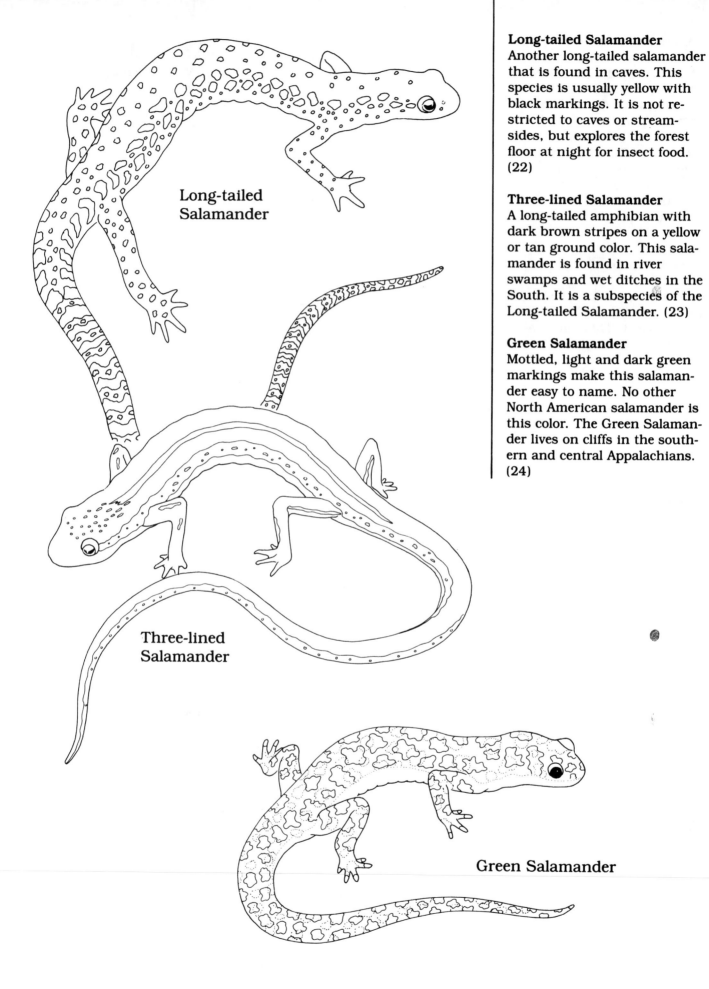

Long-tailed Salamander
Another long-tailed salamander that is found in caves. This species is usually yellow with black markings. It is not restricted to caves or streamsides, but explores the forest floor at night for insect food. (22)

Three-lined Salamander
A long-tailed amphibian with dark brown stripes on a yellow or tan ground color. This salamander is found in river swamps and wet ditches in the South. It is a subspecies of the Long-tailed Salamander. (23)

Green Salamander
Mottled, light and dark green markings make this salamander easy to name. No other North American salamander is this color. The Green Salamander lives on cliffs in the southern and central Appalachians. (24)

Long-tailed
Salamander

Three-lined
Salamander

Green Salamander

You will have to look hard for the Rubber Boa (134) and Northern Alligator Lizard (113) in the moist, humid forests of the Pacific Coast. They hide under the abundant rotting wood and thick ferns of the forest floor. The Pacific Treefrog (50) and the Red-legged Frog (47) are less often concealed and may be easier to spot. Search for the Pacific Giant Salamander (28) under logs and near water.

Pacific Northwest Forest

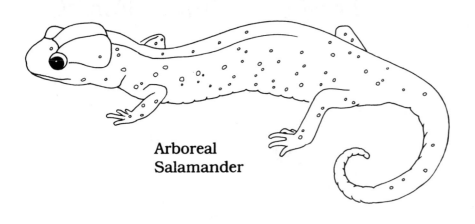

Arboreal
Salamander

Arboreal Salamander
Yellow spots mark the shiny, dark brown skin of this amphibian. It lives both in tree crevices and on the ground under rotting vegetation. Look for this salamander in live-oak woodlands on the West Coast. (25)

Oregon Slender Salamander
This slim animal's dark brown body is marked with a reddish or yellowish brown stripe. Active above ground in April or May in moist Pacific Coast woods. (26)

Mount Lyell Salamander
The shape of this salamander makes it unmistakable. The irregular gray, brown, and tan markings blend with the granite rocks of its Sierra Nevada habitat. (27)

Pacific Giant Salamander
A large salamander. This animal is shown in the Pacific Northwest Forest Scene, p. 15. Its network of irregular black spots contrasts with its brown, gray, or purplish ground color. Females lay their eggs near springs and the larvae (young) live under rocks in cold, clear streams. (28)

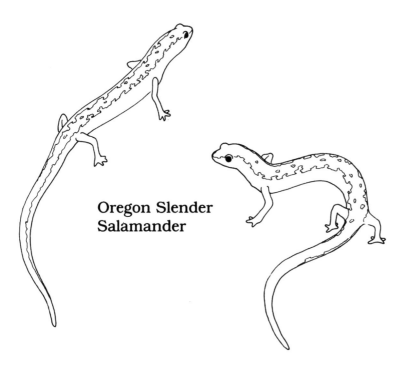

Oregon Slender
Salamander

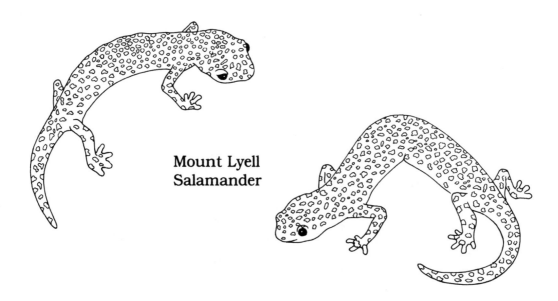

Mount Lyell
Salamander

Frogs and Toads

Frogs occur in many habitats throughout the United States. Their larvae live in water as tadpoles. These moist-skinned amphibians need wetlands, and their numbers are declining in many parts of the country due to pollution and the draining of their marshy homes.

Rough-skinned relatives of frogs, toads also need water in which to lay their eggs and develop as larvae. Toads are carnivorous as adults. Unlike frogs, they hop instead of leaping. Even though they have moist skins and are prone to water loss, toads have adapted to drier environments than frogs. They survive by burrowing or hiding beneath rocks and logs to avoid the daytime heat.

Tailed Frog
The Tailed Frog lives in cold streams of northwestern woods. Both sexes are olive, brown, gray, or reddish brown, with a pale yellow triangle on the snout. The eyestripe is dark brown. Only the male has a tail, which is used in reproduction. (29)

Greenhouse Frog
Imported from the Caribbean, these frogs are often found in gardens in the Southeast. The skin is reddish brown with lighter brown stripes. (30)

Northern Cricket Frog
A frog of northern and upland habitats. Its colors vary, but it often has a bright green body divided by dark brown markings. The legs are usually light brown. (31)

Southern Cricket Frog
Unlike its northern relative, this cricket frog inhabits river bottoms and lowland swamps in the South. The light tan body is marked with large brown blotches. The belly is light yellow. (32)

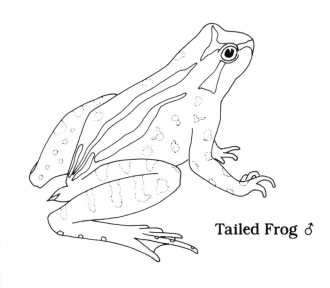

Tailed Frog ♂

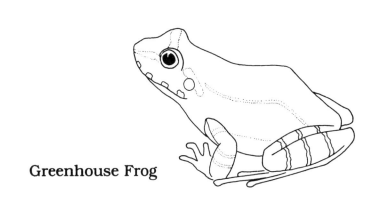

Greenhouse Frog

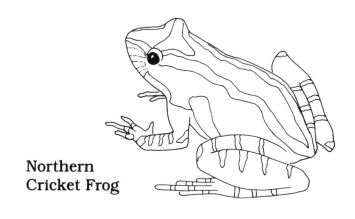

Northern
Cricket Frog

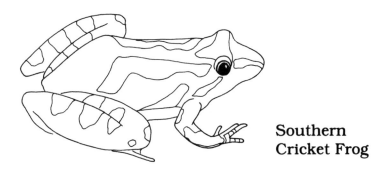

Southern
Cricket Frog

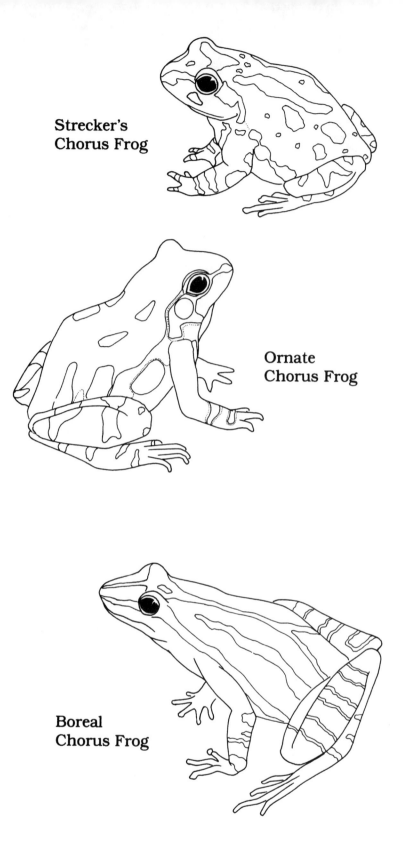

Strecker's
Chorus Frog

Ornate
Chorus Frog

Boreal
Chorus Frog

Little
Grass Frog

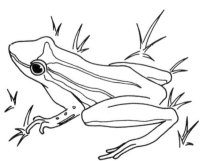

Strecker's Chorus Frog
A chubby frog with a black or dark brown stripe running from eye to shoulder. The ground color varies from gray to brown or green. Darker markings mottle the back. (33)

Ornate Chorus Frog
This frog varies in color and pattern. Both forms are shown in the Eastern Woodlands Scene on p. 27. The less colorful form (shown only in the scene) is actually more common. The "ornate" form shown here displays a green back and legs, pink sides, and a silvery white belly. The back markings are brown, while those on the sides are black. Males call during fall, winter, and spring in ponds, flooded meadows, and ditches. (34)

Boreal Chorus Frog
A subspecies of the Striped Chorus Frog. Use light and dark shades of gray, brown, or olive-green for this frog. It lives in temporary pools and has adapted to life on farms and in open areas near some cities. (35)

Little Grass Frog
The smallest frog in North America. This tiny amphibian sometimes looks transparent, and its pattern often varies. Here are two individuals to color. They may be generally greenish, pink, or reddish. The back and upper legs are often reddish. A dark stripe through the eye contrasts with a pale tan background. (36)

Carpenter Frog

A well-camouflaged frog of sphagnum bogs. Two light golden stripes mark its mottled green body. The upper lip is light yellow. (37)

Mink Frog

When rubbed, this frog's skin smells like the musky scent of a mink. Brown and yellow mottling covers the back and legs. The eardrum is bright brown in a field of bright green. A northern species, the mink frog lives in ponds, where it may travel across lily pads floating on the surface. (38)

Wood Frog

The ground color of this frog may be light tan, gray, pink, or brown. A dark eye patch stands out in light individuals but can always be seen, even in dark brown forms. The lips are light yellow. The Wood Frog usually lives in prairies or wooded areas in the United States and southern Canada. (39)

Pickerel Frog

The rather square markings on this light green or yellow frog are black or dark brown. The upper jaw has a light line. Skin-gland secretions protect this frog from being eaten by snakes. (40)

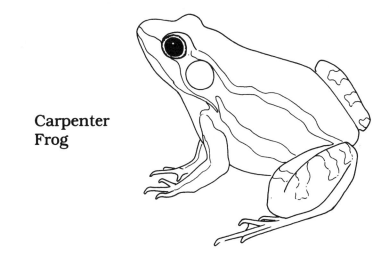

Carpenter Frog

Mink Frog

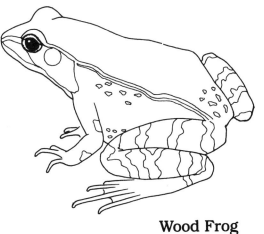

Wood Frog

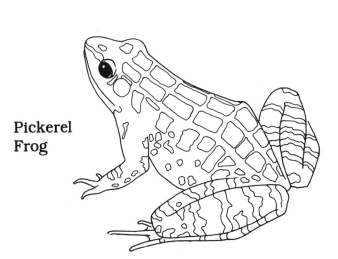

Pickerel Frog

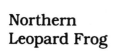

**Northern
Leopard Frog**

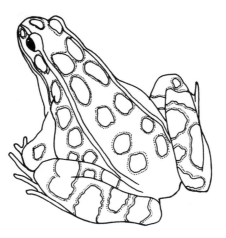

Northern Leopard Frog and Southern Leopard Frog

Both of these species of leopard frog are either brown or green, with dark brown spots. The Southern Leopard Frog has a longer snout and a light spot in the middle of the eardrum. Both species leave the water in summer and enter meadows in search of insect food. (41)

Cascades Frog

Inky black spots on its back and dark spots on its legs contrast with this amphibian's brown skin. The yellowish or cream sides blend into the yellow lower abdomen. This frog lives on mountainsides near water, occasionally near the treeline. (42)

Crawfish Frog

The dark spots on this frog are ringed with light yellow, contrasting with the yellow and dark brown body. The Crawfish Frog frequents holes made by small animals, but the holes must be wet or damp. (43)

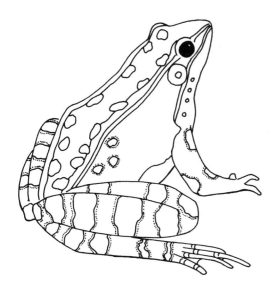

**Southern
Leopard Frog**

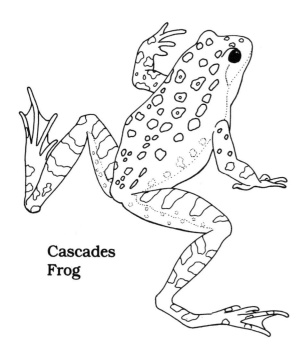

**Cascades
Frog**

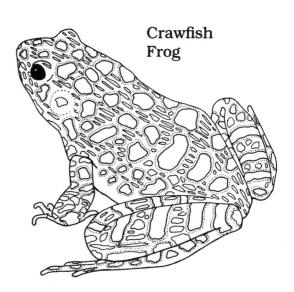

**Crawfish
Frog**

Foothill Yellow-legged Frog
A mottled brown, gray, or olive frog with a pale triangle on its snout. The yellow underside of the legs shows when the frog crawls or leaps. Sunny banks of running forest streams are the favorite haunts of this frog. It stays near water. (44)

Mountain Yellow-legged Frog
Dusky toe tips distinguish this mountain-dwelling species. It is usually gray, brown, or olive. It likes to bask on lake shores and in sunny riverside glades. (45)

Bronze Frog
A frog named for its color. The upper jaw and part of its shoulder are occasionally green, but the rest of the body is bronze. Because of its secretive nature, this frog is often hard to find. It lives in southern swamps, and is shown in the Southern Swamp Scene, p. 37. (46)

Red-legged Frog
Also appears in the Pacific Northwest Forest Scene, p. 15. A large frog of western marshes and woodland ponds. Small flecks mark the reddish brown or gray background. The red leg pattern becomes obvious when the frog moves. (47)

Bullfrog
The largest frog in North America. The basic coloring can be olive, green, or brown. Dark bands mark the legs. The chin and lower parts are white, mottled with gray. The throat is yellow in breeding males. To find Bullfrogs at night, shine a flashlight around pond edges, especially when you hear a deep *jug-o'-rum* sound. (48)

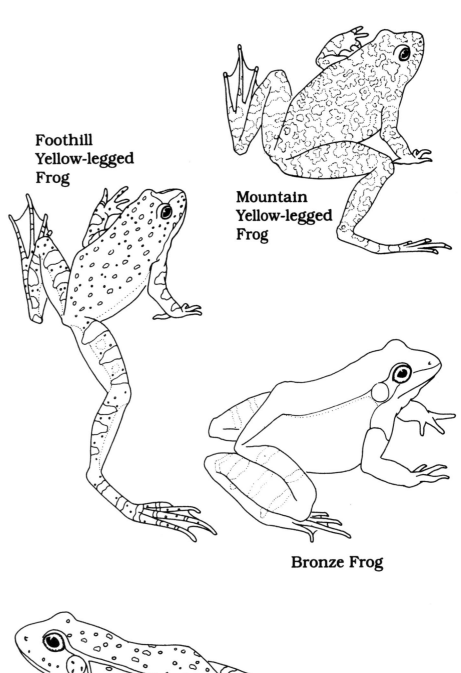

Foothill
Yellow-legged
Frog

Mountain
Yellow-legged
Frog

Bronze Frog

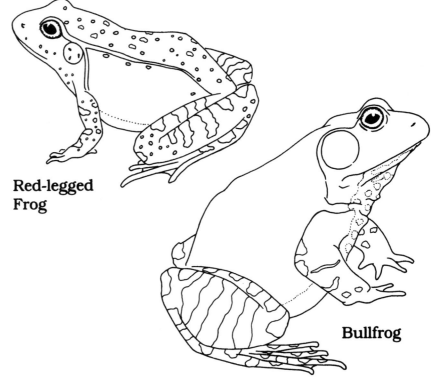

Red-legged
Frog

Bullfrog

**Barking
Frog**

**Pacific
Treefrog**

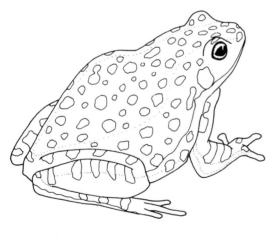

**Barking
Treefrog**

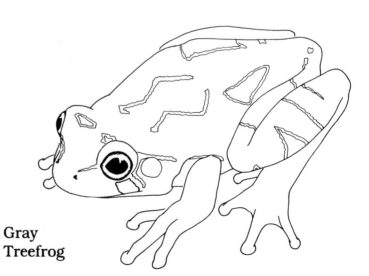

**Gray
Treefrog**

Barking Frog
A frog of extreme southern Arizona and New Mexico and central Texas. Its dark blotches often have lighter borders. The ground color is purplish gray. The male's voice sounds like a barking dog. (49)

Pacific Treefrog
Shown in the Pacific Northwest Forest Scene, p. 15. A small brown, gray, or green frog. The dark eyestripe is always present, but is sometimes difficult to see. This frog is found in a variety of Pacific Coast habitats. It frequents moist meadows and marshes in the Northwest. (50)

Barking Treefrog
A chubby, boldly marked treefrog. The dark brown spots show up against its light brown or green body. The belly may be yellow. You might hear the barking sound of its voice from above, since this frog sometimes climbs in trees. (51)

Gray Treefrog
Mottled shades of gray, brown, or green provide this frog with superb camouflage as it rests on a tree trunk or limb. Note the light mark below the eye. (52)

Pine Barrens Treefrog
This beautiful frog is rarely seen, except when it calls in spring or early summer. Lavender stripes bordered with white contrast with its brilliant green back, legs, and head. It lives in the acidic waters of the New Jersey Pine Barrens, and in many other places southward to northern Florida. (53)

Spring Peeper
A dark brown cross marks this frog's back, but the cross is not always complete. The background may be gray, brown, or olive. Most unpolluted ponds in eastern woodlands will have Spring Peepers. (54)

Squirrel Treefrog
Rain brings out the Squirrel Treefrog. It is common in gardens and tangled vegetation. This frog has a remarkable ability to change its color, so you could color it brown or green. If you choose green, make the side markings light brown. (55)

Pine Woods Treefrog
This frog inhabits coastal pine woods in southern states. It is usually deep reddish brown with vague darker markings, but may also be gray or greenish gray. (56)

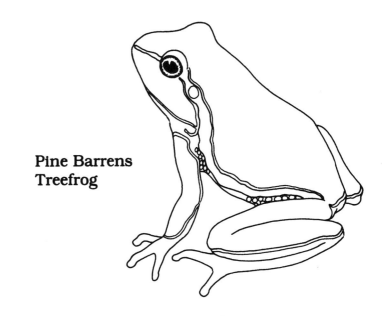

Pine Barrens
Treefrog

Spring
Peeper

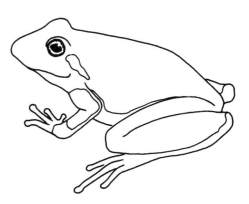

Squirrel
Treefrog

Pine Woods
Treefrog

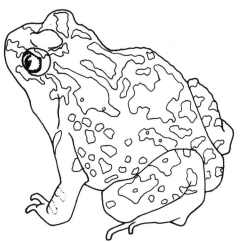

Plains
Spadefoot

Plains Spadefoot
This toad seeks drier areas of the Great Plains and usually avoids woodlands and river bottoms. It is gray or brown with a green tone. The dark gray or brown markings set off vague lighter stripes on the back. Spadefoot toads burrow into loose soil with spadelike structures on their hind feet. (57)

Eastern Spadefoot
Wavy, light yellow lines contrast with the brownish ground color of this burrowing toad. It lives in sandy eastern woodlands. (58)

Couch's Spadefoot
This toad inhabits shortgrass plains and other arid areas of the southern United States and Mexico. An irregular, dark pattern stands out against the variable background of bright greenish or brownish yellow. The male is often more greenish than the female, with the dark markings on the back fainter or even absent. (59)

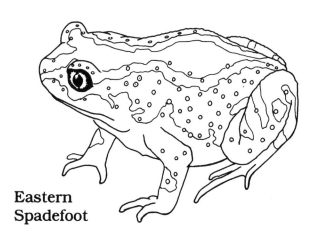

Eastern
Spadefoot

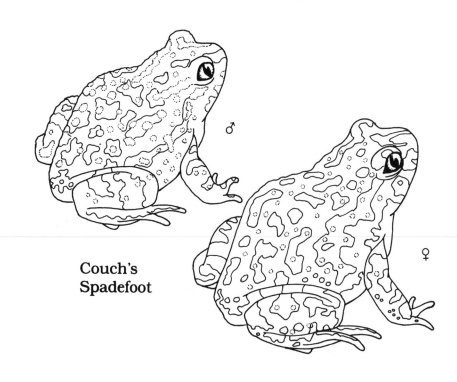

Couch's
Spadefoot

Western Spadefoot

Since it is generally darker than other spadefoot toads, color this toad in tones of gray, brown, dusky green, or almost black. Blotches of darker color show up against most of these tones. Although absent from the harshest deserts, the Western Spadefoot thrives in dry areas and alkali flats of the West. (60)

Eastern Narrow-mouthed Toad

Appearance rather than color distinguishes this small, plump toad. Color the back with gray, brown, or reddish shades. These colors are bordered by lighter stripes on the sides. This toad eats small beetles, termites, and ants. (61)

Sonoran Desert Toad

One of the largest North American toads, this toad grows up to six inches long. Its brown or olive coloring is uniform except for a white wart at each corner of its mouth. The throat is pale cream. Living near temporary and permanent water, this toad occurs throughout the arid extreme Southwest. (62)

Western Toad

The Western Toad is commonly found from sea level to high in the mountains. It often lives in western gardens. Look for the white or cream-colored stripe that runs along the dusky, gray, or greenish back. Dark blotches often tinged with red cover the warts. (63)

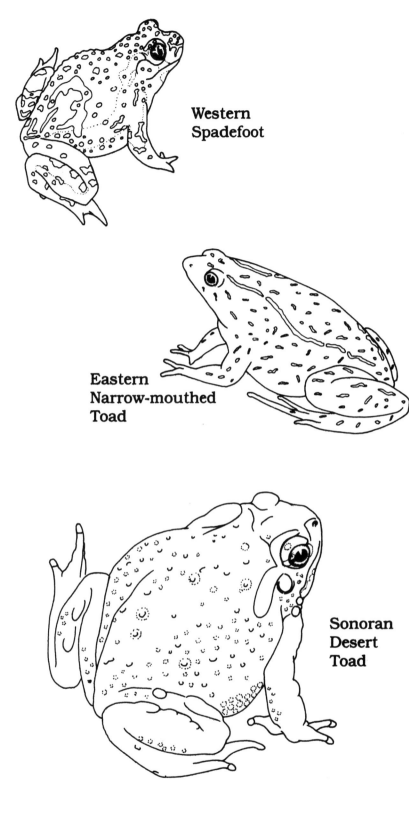

Western Spadefoot

Eastern Narrow-mouthed Toad

Sonoran Desert Toad

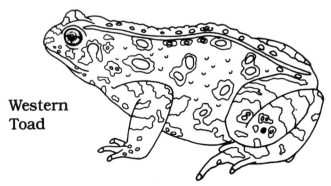

Western Toad

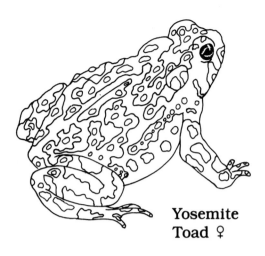

Yosemite
Toad ♀

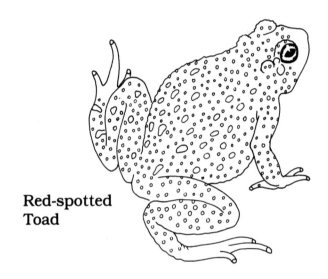

Red-spotted
Toad

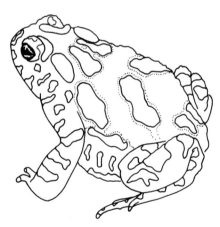

Great Plains
Toad

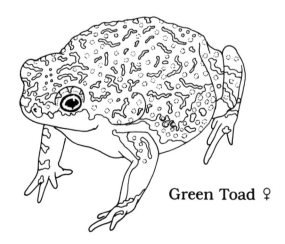

Green Toad ♀

Yosemite Toad
This black-blotched Yosemite Toad is a female. Make the ground color pale yellow. Males are yellow-green or dark olive and lack the dark markings. The Yosemite Toad has smoother skin than its close relative, the Western Toad. (64)

Red-spotted Toad
A small toad of desert oases and grasslands in the West. The light gray, olive, or reddish brown back is marked with reddish or orange warts. (65)

Great Plains Toad
This toad also appears in the Prairie Scene, p. 51. Large numbers of this species gather to breed in temporary pools in prairie or desert habitats. Their loud breeding voices may be overwhelming at close range. (66)

Green Toad
A vivid green toad with black bars or spots on its back. These markings may join to form a network. Color this female's throat cream or yellow. Males have a dark throat. Breeding depends on the summer rainy season, since the Green Toad often reproduces in temporary streams and pools formed by the rains. (67)

The eastern woodlands are home to a diverse collection of reptiles and amphibians. Here, a secretive Scarlet Kingsnake (169) hides in the leaf litter. The Oak Toad (68) is well camouflaged on the forest floor. Watch for the Eastern Box Turtle (83) as it moves through the forest clearings.

You can track down the Ornate Chorus Frog (34) by its voice during spring breeding. Two forms of this variable frog are shown here. The more common form (on the right) is reddish brown, with dark brown markings on its sides and legs. The throat and belly are light green, fading to white. The other, more colorful, form has a green back and legs, pink sides, and a silvery white belly. The back markings are brown, and the side markings are black.

Eastern Woodlands

68

83

34

169

Oak Toad

Oak Toad
Also shown in the Eastern Woodlands Scene, p. 27. A chubby little toad of southern pine woods. Its warts are red, orange, or reddish brown. The large black blotches lie in a field of pearl gray or black. A light yellowish orange or cream stripe down the middle of the back completes the markings. (68)

Woodhouse's Toad
An abundant species in Midwest grasslands and the arid Southwest. This nondescript toad is generally olive, brown, or green, with irregular darker marks. It may have one or more warts in these darker marks. (69)

American Toad
The gaily patterned female American Toad contrasts with the plain brown male. Color this female gray, olive, or brick red, with yellow or buff patches and contrasting dark spots. The warts may be yellow, orange, or red. A common toad in the Northeast, found in gardens as well as in isolated wilderness. (70)

Woodhouse's Toad

American Toad ♀

Crocodiles and Alligators

These robust, scaly reptiles are related to the extinct dinosaurs. Twenty-one species of crocodiles and their relatives occur throughout the tropical regions of the world. They are all aquatic and carnivorous. The United States has one species of crocodile and one species of alligator. You can tell them apart by the shape of their snouts — the crocodile's is long and tapering, while the alligator's is broadly rounded. In the crocodile, a long tooth protrudes from the lower jaw when the mouth is closed. Both reptiles will emerge onto land and can move quite quickly. Alligators are frequently seen basking in warm, sunlit waters.

American Crocodile

The adult crocodile is rather uniform in color, usually dark greenish gray or tan-gray. The young are gray or greenish gray with narrow black crossbands or rows of spots. These huge reptiles live in salty or brackish water around Biscayne Bay and the Florida Keys. Once widespread, crocodiles are now rare. The female lays her eggs in sand and usually leaves them to hatch alone. She may return to the nest at night. (71)

American Alligator

Generally black. The yellow crossbands of young individuals may be vaguely visible in older alligators. The species frequents river swamps, lakes, and marshes in the southeastern United States. They often bask below the surface with only their eyes and snout above water. Females guard their nests until the eggs hatch. (72)

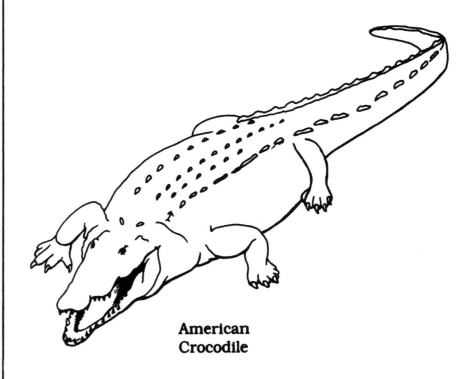

American
Crocodile

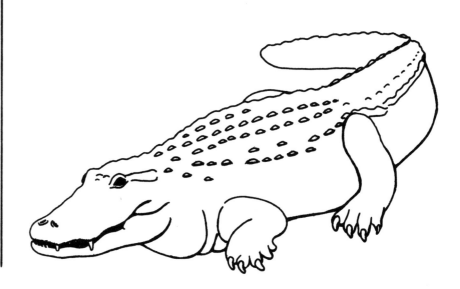

American
Alligator

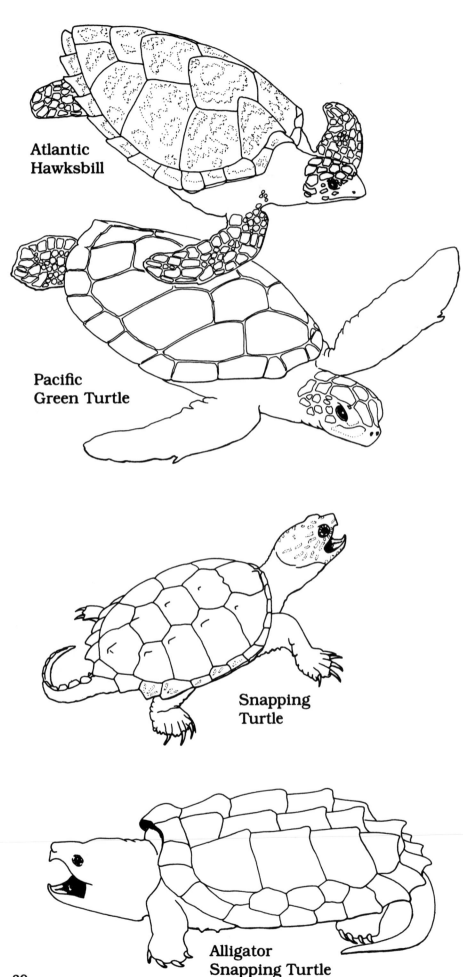

Atlantic Hawksbill

Pacific Green Turtle

Snapping Turtle

Alligator Snapping Turtle

Turtles

Turtles are easy to recognize by their protective shells. They are found in many parts of the United States. These reptiles have adapted to life both on land and in the water. The land-dwelling species of the Southwest are called tortoises. Basking is a common behavior in both land-dwelling and aquatic species. Females dig a hole on land and lay hard-shelled eggs. The hatchlings must work their way to the surface.

The parts of a turtle's shell are shown on p. 5.

Atlantic Hawksbill
Brown and yellow colors mix on this turtle's head, flippers, and carapace (upperside of the shell). The species was once hunted for this "tortoiseshell" pattern. It is found in warmer parts of the Atlantic, but also strays into southern New England waters. (73)

Pacific Green Turtle
This subspecies of the Green Turtle is a large marine turtle of the open Pacific. Females come ashore to lay eggs. The back is olive, often with no pattern, while the head is olive with scales outlined in yellow. This turtle is now rare, although old records report it was once common in San Diego Bay. (74)

Snapping Turtle
This animal is generally mud-colored, brown to black. It burrows under mud in many permanent bodies of water. This turtle becomes aggressive when caught on land. It is a favorite food in some sections of the country. (75)

Alligator Snapping Turtle
A very large, freshwater turtle. Color it brown. This turtle wiggles a pink "lure" on the floor of its mouth to attract fish as it lies on the bottom of a pond or river with its mouth open. (76)

Eastern Painted Turtle

This subspecies of the Painted Turtle is often seen basking on logs near water. The dark carapace has red and black margins. The head has two yellow spots on each side. The large scutes (plates) of the carapace have light edges. (77)

Southern Painted Turtle

This subspecies has a broad red stripe down the carapace, and a yellow plastron (underside of the shell). Yellow separates the scutes on the carapace. (78)

Red-bellied Turtle

This animal also appears in the Southern Swamp Scene, p. 37. Broad red markings on the carapace of the female separate less regular yellow lines. Both colors contrast with the dark brown background. Narrow yellow stripes mark the head. Males are dark with faint, irregular markings. (79)

River Cooter

Light concentric circles mark the dark scutes on the carapace. The C-shaped marking on the second scute is characteristic of this species. The head is striped black and yellow. This turtle lives only in rivers that arise from the Piedmont and flow to the Atlantic Coast. (80)

Slider

Another black and yellow turtle that disappears into water at the slightest sign of danger. Distinct brown markings on the plastron and light, irregular, C-shaped lines on the carapace are field marks that help identify it. (81)

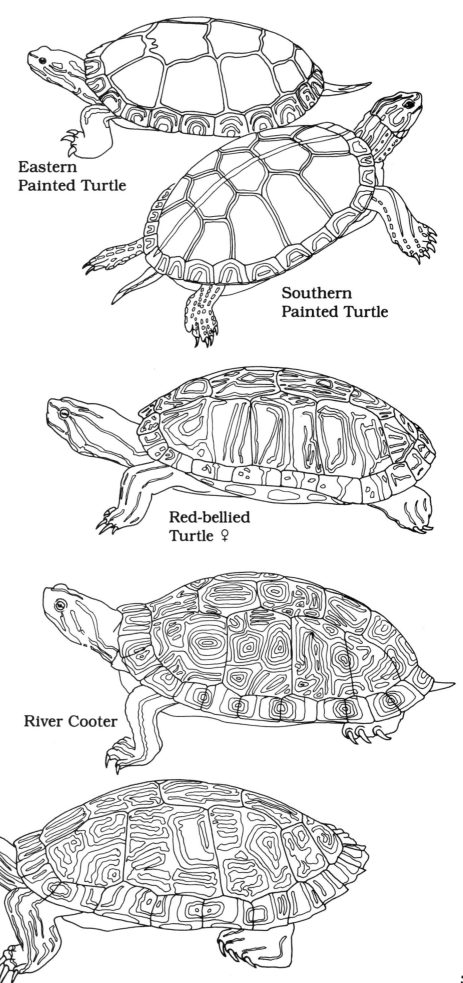

Eastern Painted Turtle

Southern Painted Turtle

Red-bellied Turtle ♀

River Cooter

Slider

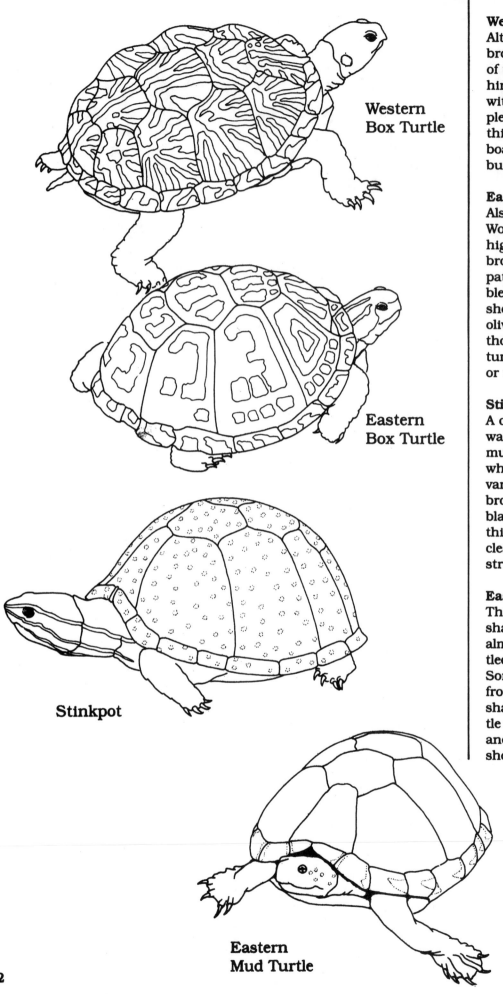

Western
Box Turtle

Eastern
Box Turtle

Stinkpot

Eastern
Mud Turtle

Western Box Turtle
Alternating yellow and dark brown markings grace the shell of this species. The plastron is hinged, allowing the turtle to withdraw into its shell completely. Found on the prairie, this turtle seeks shelter under boards or rocks, or in self-made burrows. (82)

Eastern Box Turtle
Also shown in the Eastern Woodlands Scene, p. 27. The high shell distinguishes this brown and yellow turtle. The pattern can be extremely variable, and both upper and lower shells may be yellow, orange, or olive on black or brown. Although they live on land, these turtles sometimes soak in mud or water for long periods. (83)

Stinkpot
A common turtle of eastern waters. It is named for the musky secretion it produces when captured. The carapace varies from black to light olive-brown and may be spotted with black. Green algae may obscure this coloring, but the head will clearly show two light yellow stripes. (84)

Eastern Mud Turtle
This turtle comes in various shades of brown, from olive to almost black. Its head is mottled or streaked with yellow. Some individuals may wander from the protection of their shallow-water haunts. This turtle will tolerate brackish water and can be found on many offshore islands. (85)

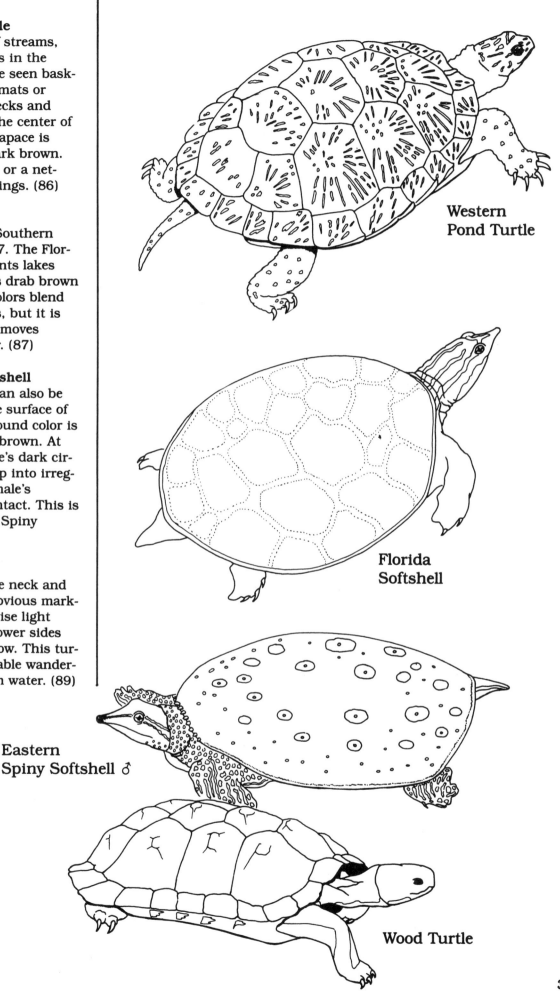

Western Pond Turtle
An aquatic turtle of streams, ponds, and marshes in the West. It can often be seen basking on logs, cattail mats or mudbanks. Dark flecks and lines radiate from the center of each scute. The carapace is generally olive or dark brown. The head has spots or a network of black markings. (86)

Florida Softshell
Also shown in the Southern Swamp Scene, p. 37. The Florida Softshell frequents lakes and quiet rivers. Its drab brown or brownish gray colors blend with sandy bottoms, but it is easy to see when it moves through clear water. (87)

Eastern Spiny Softshell
A river turtle that can also be seen floating on the surface of quiet lakes. The ground color is olive-gray to yellow-brown. At maturity, the female's dark circular spots break up into irregular patches. The male's markings remain intact. This is a subspecies of the Spiny Softshell. (88)

Wood Turtle
Orange areas on the neck and legs are the most obvious markings on this otherwise light brown turtle. The lower sides are tinged with yellow. This turtle is quite comfortable wandering on land far from water. (89)

Western
Pond Turtle

Florida
Softshell

Eastern
Spiny Softshell ♂

Wood Turtle

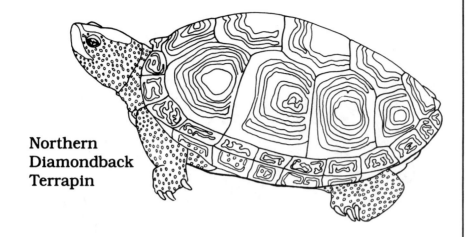

Northern Diamondback Terrapin

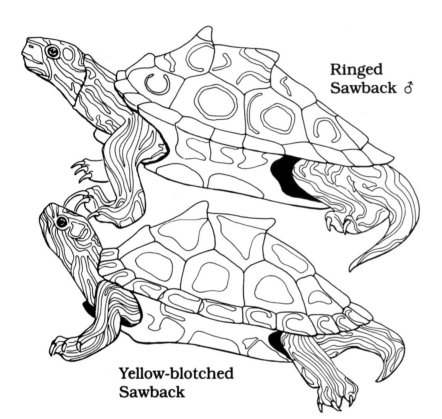

Ringed Sawback ♂

Yellow-blotched Sawback

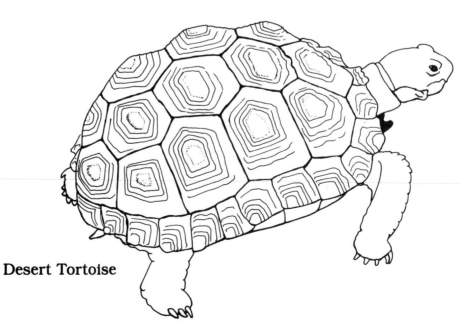

Desert Tortoise

Northern Diamondback Terrapin
Pattern and color vary greatly in this species. The terrapin shown here has dark rings in a field of light gray. The plastron is light yellow. This turtle lives in brackish coastal waters. (90)

Ringed Sawback
Broad red rings mark the brown carapace of this male turtle. A relative of the map turtles, the Ringed Sawback has black and yellow stripes on its head, legs, and tail. A bright yellow spot occurs just behind the eye. This turtle mainly eats insects and mollusks. (91)

Yellow-blotched Sawback
This turtle has solid areas of yellow on its carapace. The head, legs, and tail are striped, as in map turtles. The carapace is ridged like a saw. This species is found only in the Pascagoula River system in Mississippi. (92)

Desert Tortoise
Also shown in the Desert Scene, p. 64. A brown or tan carapace and gray legs and tail distinguish this tortoise. It emerges from its burrow in sandy soil to feed on grass, leaves, and berries. It is active in the early morning, before the day becomes too hot. (93)

Lizards

Often glimpsed as a rapid movement on dry rocks and tree trunks, lizards are abundant in the tropics and many temperate regions. Like other reptiles, they are "cold-blooded" animals, and often bask in the sun to raise their body temperature. Many lizards are well camouflaged, with patterns that blend with their surroundings. Their scaly skin is mottled chiefly in earthy tones, although males of many species show bright colors during the breeding season.

Western Banded Gecko
Look for a pale form against the rocks when searching for this gecko at night in its desert habitat. The dark chocolate bands lighten to pink in their centers. The bands alternate with yellow bands along the tail and body. These areas break up into a blotched pattern with age. (94)

Texas Banded Gecko
The brown bands on the Texas Banded Gecko are broader than the yellow stripes between them, and are often spotted with darker brown. This lizard can be seen at night on roads and rocks in arid parts of Texas and New Mexico. (95)

Mediterranean Gecko
Introduced into North America, this gecko is found on houses and other buildings in the Gulf Coast states. Its skin color varies from pinkish ivory to light yellow or white. The larger wartlike bumps on its body and legs may be dark brown or gray, while the smaller markings are light yellow or white. It is active at night and catches insects around lights and screen doors. (96)

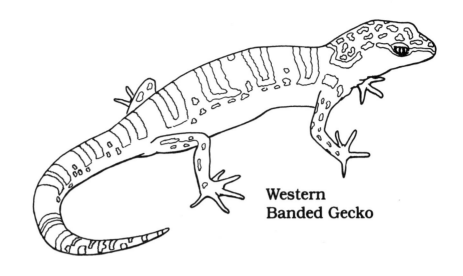

Western Banded Gecko

Texas Banded Gecko

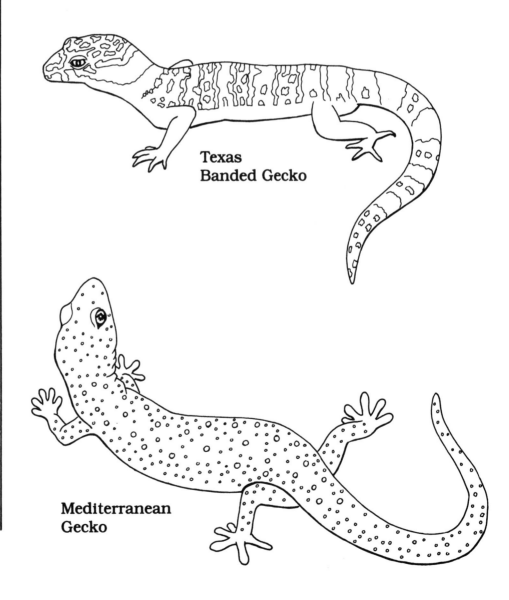

Mediterranean Gecko

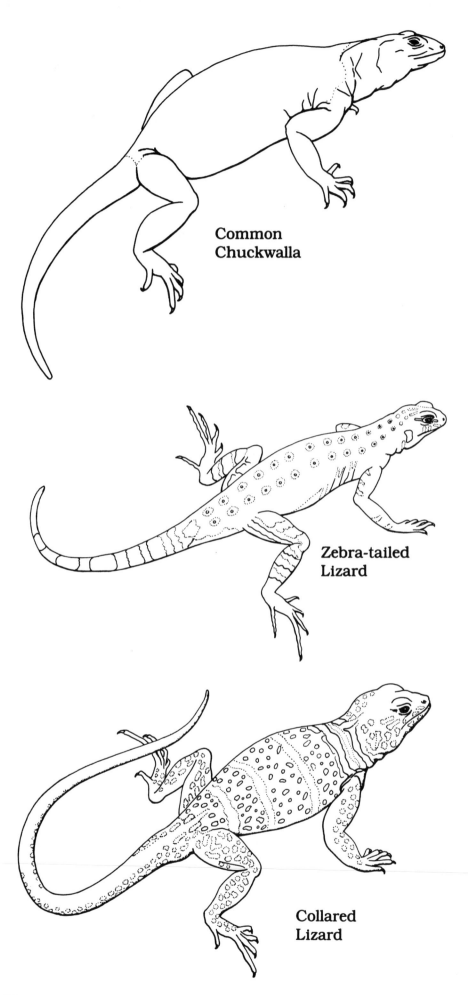

Common Chuckwalla

Zebra-tailed Lizard

Collared Lizard

Common Chuckwalla

The Common Chuckwalla is a large, plant-eating lizard that feeds on a variety of desert plants. This dark-bodied animal has loose folds of skin on its neck and sides. The male tends to be darker brown to blackish on its head and reddish or gray on its sides and tail. Late morning is a good time to look for these animals as they sprawl on a rock in the sun. When alarmed, they hide in crevices among the rocks and gulp air to expand their bodies and wedge themselves in place. (97)

Zebra-tailed Lizard

Black crossbands on the tail give this reptile its common name. The back has a series of white markings on a gray background. The sides are usually lemon yellow. The male has a pair of black bars in a blue patch on each side of the body. These bars are especially conspicuous when the lizard flattens its sides. Long, slender legs and a slender body adapt this lizard well for running across the open areas of its desert habitat. (98)

Collared Lizard

A large head, long tail, and bright markings distinguish the Collared Lizard. It has a distinct black collar across its shoulders and broad, light yellow crossbands and dots on its back and sides. The ground color on the upper surfaces is olive, pale brown, or light tan, and varies according to the place this lizard lives, and also its sex or age. This color blends into blue or green on the legs and sides. Like other fast-moving lizards, this animal lives in sparsely vegetated rock gullies and arid mountain slopes. It can be seen jumping from rock to rock or running on its rear legs with the tail raised. (99)

The warm, watery areas of this southern habitat are ideally suited for amphibians and water-loving reptiles. The Bronze Frog (46) can be found among fallen tree limbs. A basking Eastern Cottonmouth (180) enjoys the sun on a floating log, while a Red-bellied Turtle (79) and a Florida Softshell (87) hunt in the waters below.

Southern Swamp

46

180

87

79

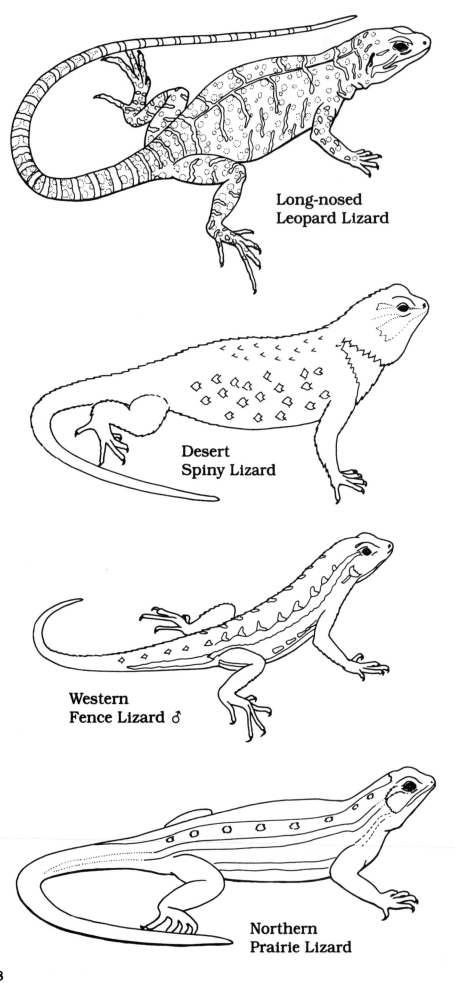

**Long-nosed
Leopard Lizard**

**Desert
Spiny Lizard**

**Western
Fence Lizard ♂**

**Northern
Prairie Lizard**

Long-nosed Leopard Lizard
Leopard-like spots camouflage this lizard as it lies in wait for prey in the mottled shade of sparse bunch grass or sagebrush. The spots usually show up clearly against the light gray or brown background, but in some darker individuals the spots are concealed and only the light stripes show. During the breeding season, females develop reddish spots on their sides. (100)

Desert Spiny Lizard
A black area on each side of the neck marks this stocky lizard. The ground color varies from straw or yellowish brown to brownish gray, with occasional darker scales. The sides are tinged with rust. The male has blue markings on the throat and belly which are absent in the female. This lizard lives in semi-arid habitats and avoids high elevations. It also occurs along dry streambeds. It is a good climber, but is also found in fallen logs and rodent burrows. (101)

Western Fence Lizard
A common lizard in the western United States, often seen on fenceposts, woodpiles and the sides of buildings. It is black, gray, or brown, with a blotched pattern. The backs of the limbs are yellow or orange. The male, shown here, has a blue belly and throat patches that show up clearly, especially when flattened in display to females or rival males. This adaptable lizard lives in many western environments, but is not found in the desert. (102)

Northern Prairie Lizard
Bold, pale-colored stripes contrast with the light reddish or reddish brown ground color. Dark spots border this lighter area. This subspecies of the Eastern Fence Lizard occupies a variety of habitats, from farmland to stabilized sand dunes and open prairies. (103)

Crevice Spiny Lizard
Black and white bands around the tail and a black collar mark this stocky, large-scaled lizard. The collar is bordered by white. The back color varies from gray to olive or red. Young lizards have bands across the back that become faded with age. An elusive animal, this reptile hides among the crevices of its rocky habitats in the Southwest. (104)

Sagebrush Lizard
Small scales give this lizard a smooth-skinned appearance. The gray or dark brown back is marked with blotches that extend onto the limbs and form a bar on each shoulder. This pattern is sometimes broken by light stripes along the sides. Males have blue patches on each side of the belly. Females have little or no blue. This lizard is named for its most common habitat, but it also lives in pine and fir forests, piñon-juniper woodland, and coastal river bottoms as well as in sagebrush. A ground-dweller, it needs plant cover for protection and open ground for hunting its insect prey. (105)

Northern Fence Lizard
A slender, gray or brown lizard. Males are uniform in color above and have a bright blue throat patch bordered by black. Females have dark, wavy cross-bands on the upper surfaces. Both sexes have a dark line running along the rear of the thigh. This slender lizard climbs trees and fences easily, especially when startled. It occurs throughout the southern and eastern U.S. Look for it in open, sunny places as it basks or hunts for insects. (106)

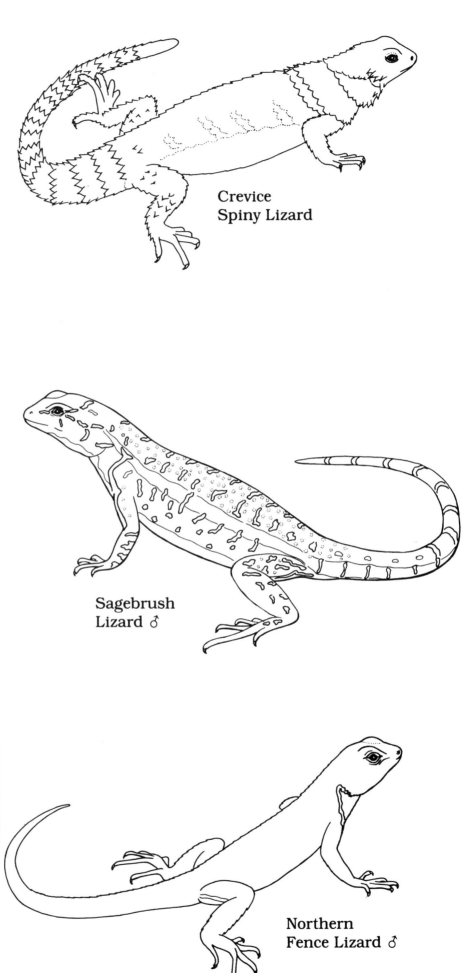

Crevice
Spiny Lizard

Sagebrush
Lizard ♂

Northern
Fence Lizard ♂

39

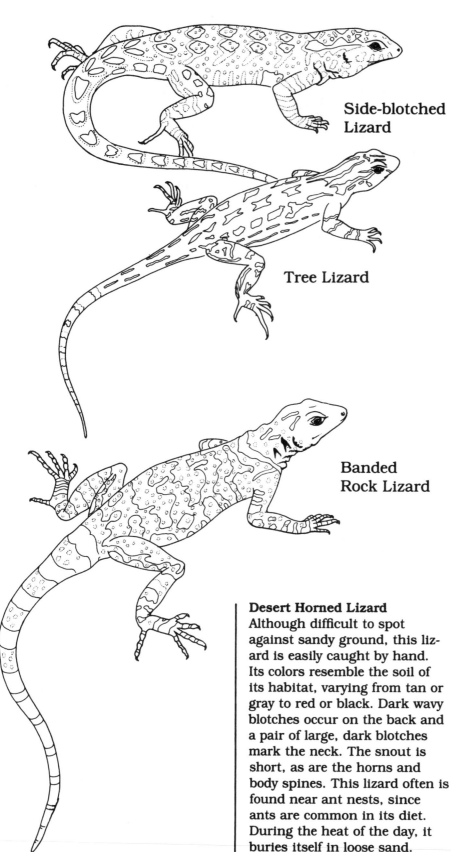

Side-blotched Lizard

Tree Lizard

Banded Rock Lizard

Side-blotched Lizard
An abundant lizard in arid and semi-arid regions of the West (see the Desert Scene, p. 64). The brown ground color is speckled with lighter patches. Males may be tinged with pale blue in the light phase. A distinctive black blotch occurs behind each forelimb. Darker, paired markings on the back become joined on the slender tail. This lizard is active during the day and can live in a variety of habitats. Look for it on the ground around plants or on exposed rock surfaces. (107)

Tree Lizard
Dark markings against a brown, gray, tan, or sandy background camouflage this wary lizard. The tail is rust-colored. Males have a blue belly and a blue, greenish, or yellow throat patch. This lizard is found on trees and rocks, often along streambeds in the Southwest. (108)

Banded Rock Lizard
You can recognize the Banded Rock Lizard from a distance as it moves over rocks and tree trunks with outstretched limbs and swinging hindquarters. Black tail bands give this lizard its name. A dark collar marking contrasts with the olive or gray body, which is dotted with blue or white spots on wavy crossbands. Watch for this reptile in desert canyons in extreme southern California. (109)

Desert Horned Lizard
Although difficult to spot against sandy ground, this lizard is easily caught by hand. Its colors resemble the soil of its habitat, varying from tan or gray to red or black. Dark wavy blotches occur on the back and a pair of large, dark blotches mark the neck. The snout is short, as are the horns and body spines. This lizard often is found near ant nests, since ants are common in its diet. During the heat of the day, it buries itself in loose sand. Watch for this lizard as it basks on warm rocks or along roadsides, in the morning or late afternoon. (110)

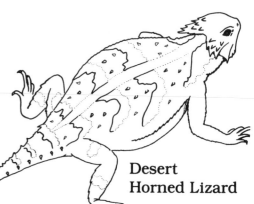

Desert Horned Lizard

Southern Alligator Lizard
A lizard of moist habitats in foothills and higher elevations. It may live near streams and springs in the drier parts of its range. The upper surfaces vary from brown or gray to reddish or yellow, with dark crossbands on the back and tail. Dark bars on the sides are spotted with white. Note the distinct fold low on each side of the body. Aided by its prehensile (grasping) tail, this agile lizard sometimes climbs bushes in search of insect prey. Secretive, it often hides among dense plant growth and may be seen in piles of logs and trash around houses. (111)

Panamint Alligator Lizard
Broad, brown crossbands on a light yellow background distinguish this alligator lizard. Like other alligator lizards, it has a skin fold along the lower sides of its body. Found under dense vegetation and rocks, this reptile lives only in the Panamint, Nelson, White, and Inyo Mountains of California. (112)

Northern Alligator Lizard
This animal also appears in the Pacific Northwest Forest Scene, p. 15. A skin fold separates the pale underside from the olive, greenish, or bluish back. The dark barring is heavier on the sides and irregular on the back. This lizard bears live young and is found in cool, damp woodlands in northwestern areas up to 10,500 feet. Look for it under logs, but be sure to carefully replace any logs or rocks overturned during your search. (113)

California Legless Lizard
Dark lines along the back and belly interrupt the pale upperside and yellow underside of this lizard. This lizard looks shiny because of its smooth scales. It hides by day under sparse vegetation in areas with loose soil or sand, and emerges at night. (114)

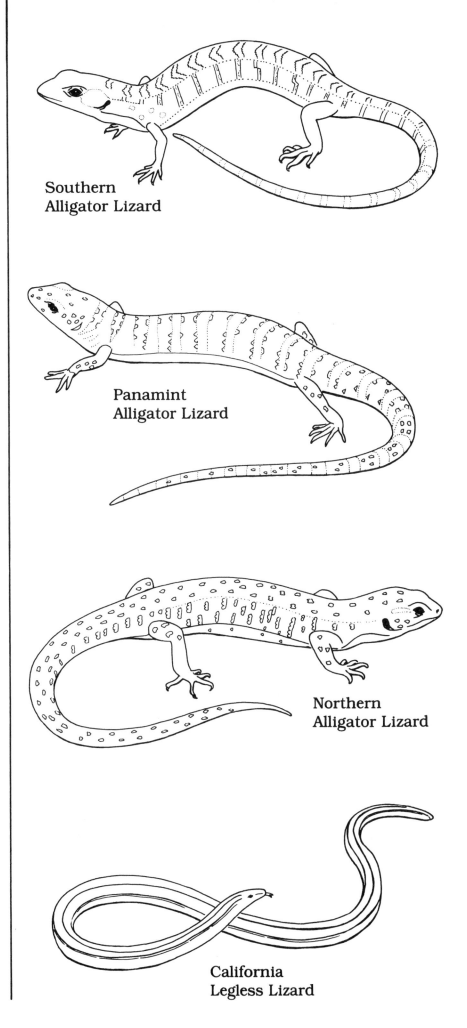

Southern
Alligator Lizard

Panamint
Alligator Lizard

Northern
Alligator Lizard

California
Legless Lizard

Gila Monster

A pattern of broad, dark bands or a network of blotches contrasts with a pink or orange background. This pattern extends onto the blunt, fat tail of this large lizard. Relatively slow-moving, Gila Monsters are often active at dusk. They feed on bird and reptile eggs and small mammals. The venom from glands in the lower jaw provides defense and may be used to subdue prey. Despite their name, these lizards are not dangerous unless handled. (115)

Green Anole

The pink throat fan, green color, and small size make this lizard easy to recognize. Individuals can change color from green to mottled or brown. Abundant in the Southeast, they frequent trees and fenceposts. Easily seen during the day, you may also spot them at night by shining a flashlight on them as they rest on shrubs and other vegetation. (116)

Northern Short-horned Lizard

This is a subspecies of the Short-horned Lizard. Generally colored like the soil on which it lives, this lizard has pairs of dark blotches along its brown or gray back. You can recognize this lizard by its short, stubby horns. It bears live young in the summer. This lizard is found throughout much of the West in a variety of habitats (from forests to dry sandy areas). Short-horned Lizards feed mainly on ants, but will eat other arthropods. (117)

Flat-tailed Horned Lizard

In this horned lizard, a dark line runs down the middle of the pale gray, buff, or reddish brown back and extends to the base of the flattened tail. The color of the back varies with the color of the lizard's habitat, windblown sand. When disturbed, this animal runs at great speed or may flatten itself against the ground or bury itself in loose sand, using sideways movements. (118)

Gila Monster

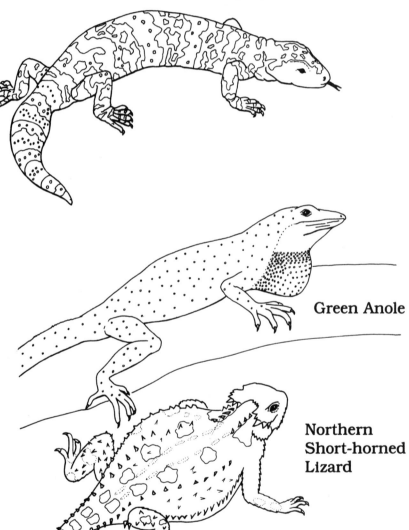

Green Anole

Northern Short-horned Lizard

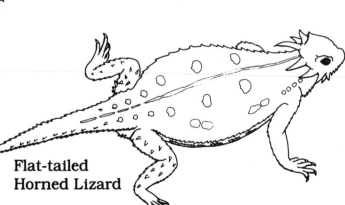

Flat-tailed Horned Lizard

Slender Glass Lizard

The movable eyelids tell you this legless lizard is not a snake. Although it moves actively when handled, a glass lizard feels less supple than a snake. The tail is fragile and will readily snap off or shatter; when it grows back, it is a different color. This lizard's markings vary with age. The medium-sized individual shown has a dark stripe down the middle of its pale yellow back, and a series of fine dark stripes on its sides, below a groove. (119)

Eastern Glass Lizard

The underside of this greenish lizard may turn yellow in older adults. Each dorsal scale has a small white marking. Irregular white markings occur on the neck. Unlike the Slender Glass Lizard, this lizard has no distinct stripe down the middle of the back. Watch for this lizard in the early morning in wet meadows, where it hunts for insects and snails. (120)

Southwestern Earless Lizard

This brilliantly colored lizard is a subspecies of the Greater Earless Lizard. The male has two broad, black, crescent-shaped marks on each side. The foreparts are gray with orange markings, and the hind legs and tail are mottled greenish. The head is generally gray in both sexes. This active lizard lives in rocky, arid flats and streambeds of the extreme Southwest. (121)

Texas Earless Lizard

Another subspecies of the Greater Earless Lizard. This lizard's general color varies from gray to reddish brown, depending on its habitat. Light flecks show against all colors. Intense black bars on the underside of the tail can be seen when the lizard raises its tail while running. Black crescents on the sides just in front of the hind limbs lie in a field of orange that blends to blue on the belly. This lizard lives in rocky streambeds, gravelly flats, and limestone cliffs. (122)

Slender
Glass Lizard

Eastern
Glass Lizard

Southwestern
Earless Lizard ♂

Texas
Earless Lizard

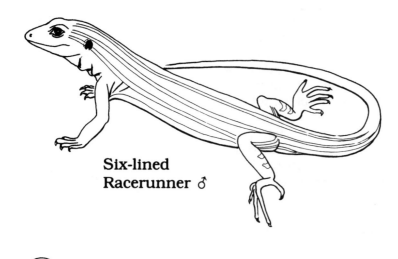

Six-lined Railerunner ♂

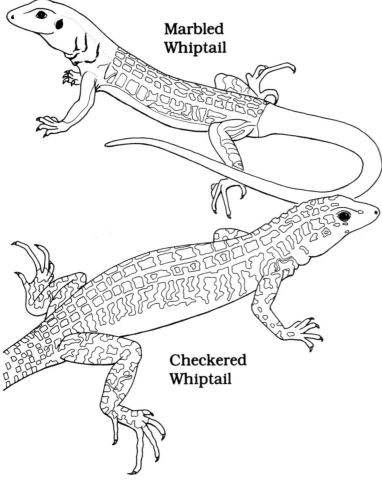

Marbled
Whiptail

Checkered
Whiptail

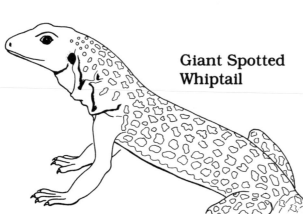

Giant Spotted
Whiptail

Six-lined Racerunner
The only whiptail lizard found in the eastern U.S. The body is slender, with six to eight light stripes. The broad, dark stripe on each side is unspotted. The hind parts and tail are light brown. In the male, the throat and belly are blue or green. In the western part of this lizard's range, the foreparts are green. (123)

Marbled Whiptail
This lizard's back and sides have a network of irregular stripes and spots against a gray, tan, brown, or yellowish background. The head and shoulders are often plain olive or brown, and the tail is dark brown. The throat may be flushed with pink, and rust patches may occur on the sides of the belly. This subspecies of the Western Whiptail lives in sparsely vegetated, dry areas of the West. (124)

Checkered Whiptail
Bold, black spots separated by light stripes of yellowish to cream cover the upper surfaces. Dark bars mark the sides of this long, slender lizard. Scattered spots on the throat and chest show against white areas. Males of this species are extremely rare. Females can reproduce without males, by cloning a batch of eggs in early summer which hatches in August. Like other whiptails, this lizard is very active in open, arid areas where its running ability helps it capture prey. (125)

Giant Spotted Whiptail
Large, pale yellow to orange spots are arranged in even rows across the reddish, brown, or gray upper surfaces. These spots fade on the tail, forelimbs, and head. The underparts are white or gray, and the head and back are reddish brown. The young have stripes that fade with age. This lizard lives in arid and semi-arid regions of the Southwest, especially near streambeds. (126)

Ground Skink
A small, secretive reptile found among leaf litter in southern woodlands. A dark line along the side is the only marking on the smooth, golden brown to dark brown body. This lizard searches for insects on the forest floor. (127)

Great Plains Skink
Adults of this species may vary in color depending on where they live. Their ground color may be gray, light tan, or olive-brown above, and pale yellow below. Black or brown spots cover the back and sides, and light salmon spots mark the sides. The young are black with a dark blue tail and orange and white markings on the head. The largest skink in the United States, this species is found in grasslands and woodlands of the Great Plains, and ranges into the mountains. The female broods her nest of eggs beneath rocks or other cover in May and June. (128)

Western Skink
Dark brown above and light below. A light stripe along the upper side is edged with black above and bordered below by a black stripe. These stripes extend onto the tail, which is bright blue in the young and rust, brown, or dull blue in adults. The tail is easily lost, which can allow the skink to escape when attacked. Look for this reptile under rocks and logs in grasslands or forests in the West, especially near streams. (129)

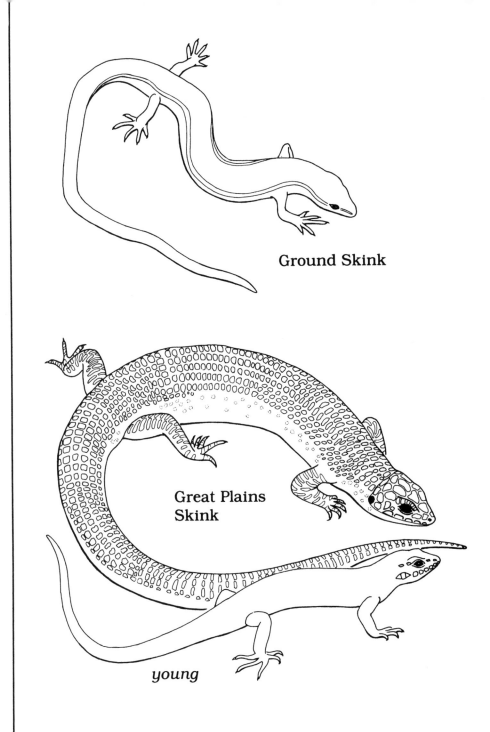

Ground Skink

Great Plains Skink

young

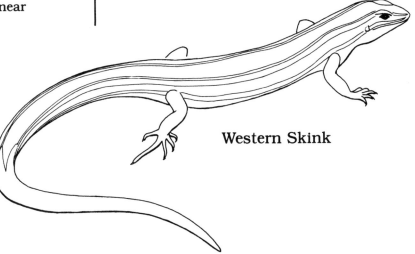

Western Skink

Mole Skink subspecies

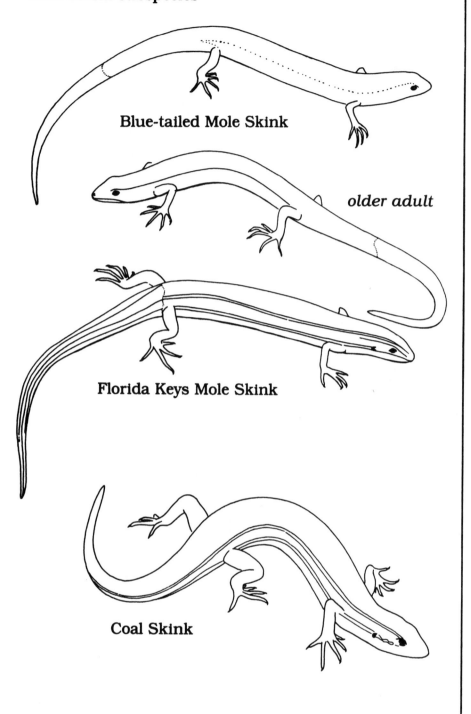

Blue-tailed Mole Skink

older adult

Florida Keys Mole Skink

Coal Skink

Five-lined Skink

young ♂

Mole Skink
A slender skink with short legs, well adapted for tunnelling. It lives in well-drained, sandy soil in the Southeast. The Blue-tailed subspecies can be recognized by the colorful tail, which is bright blue in the young and fades to light blue or salmon in older adults. The body is light to dark brown above and darker on the sides. In the Florida Keys subspecies, the tail is bright red and striped with black, and the body is dark, striped with yellow. (130)

Coal Skink
This light brown reptile has a broad, black side stripe edged with light yellow stripes extending onto the tail. Males sometimes develop a reddish color on the head. The young (not shown) have a blue tail. Found in various places throughout the Midwest and East, the Coal Skink prefers humid rocky hillsides with access to shallow water. When threatened, this skink hides in the water beneath rocks. (131)

Five-lined Skink
This animal also appears in the Prairie Scene, p. 51. Young Five-lined Skinks have blue tails, and five light stripes against a dark brown background. These stripes fade with age, especially in males. The male's lower head and chin are reddish. This animal prefers damp places, rotting logs, abandoned woodpiles, and decaying trees where it hunts for insects. (132)

Snakes

An elongated body and scaled skin characterize this highly specialized and widespread group of reptiles. All of our species lack limbs, external ear openings, and eyelids. Snakes occur in many areas of the world. They are well adapted to life on the ground, and some climb in plants and trees. Some live partly or completely in the water. Many have developed venom for defense and hunting prey. Most species lay eggs, but some bear live young.

Western Blind Snake

A small, slender snake, either brown, gray, or pink above and a lighter color below. The smooth, round-edged scales give the snake a shiny appearance. The eyes are vestigial, and can no longer see. The tail ends in a spine. This snake is rarely seen since it lives in crevices or in loose, damp soil. (133)

Rubber Boa

Also shown in the Pacific Northwest Forest Scene, p. 15. Related to boa constrictors and pythons, this thick-bodied snake has a tail shaped like its head. When alarmed, the snake may roll into a ball with its head protected inside. The body is plain brown or pink-brown above and yellowish below. The skin is smooth and shiny and forms into folds when the body is bent. The Rubber Boa lives mainly on the ground, but may swim and climb. (134)

Rosy Boa

The Rosy Boa's head is little wider than the rest of its sturdy body. The ground color on the upperside is slaty or beige. Brown stripes and blotches mark the sides. The underside is lighter and blotched with gray. This snake is seen at dusk or at night in rocky, arid parts of the Southwest. (135)

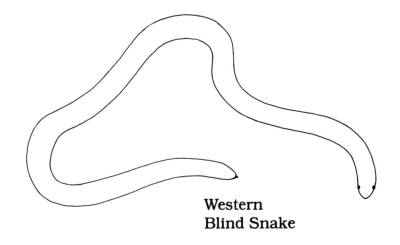

Western
Blind Snake

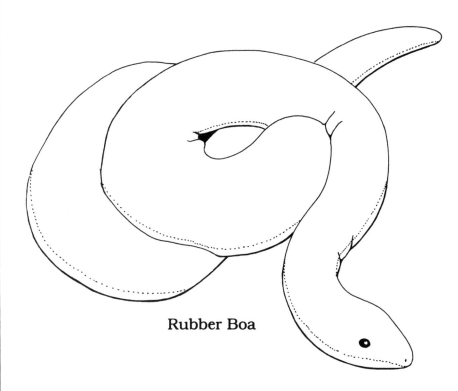

Rubber Boa

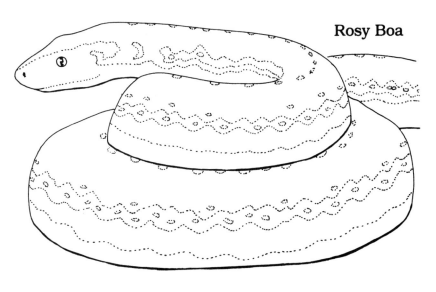

Rosy Boa

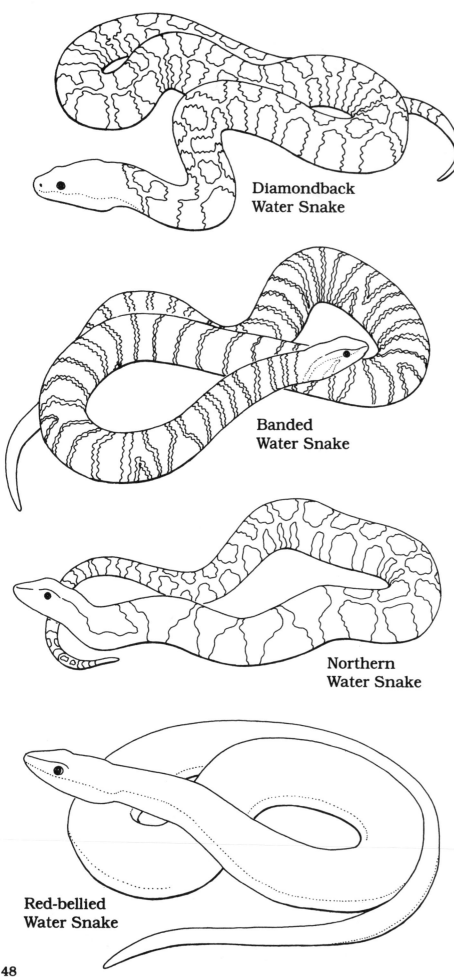

Diamondback Water Snake
A robust snake with light, irregular, diamond-shaped markings on its back and sides. These marks are separated by dark brown, chainlike areas. The belly and lower jaw are yellow. This snake stays near streams in arid areas. It hunts fishes and frogs, and is sometimes mistaken for the Cottonmouth, p. 61. (136)

Banded Water Snake
Red and yellow crossbands separated by black extend the length of this snake. A dark eyestripe marks the head. Coloring varies; the crossbands may be red, brown, or black, and the ground color may be gray, tan, or yellow. Older individuals are darker. This snake frequents fresh water, where it can be seen basking on logs or on low tree branches hanging over the water. (137)

Northern Water Snake
This subspecies of the Common Water Snake is the only large water snake in the north-central and northeastern states. It is highly variable. Large, dark brownish red markings extend across the back and sides and are separated by light yellow areas. The underside is white or yellow. This reptile is common in all unpolluted watery environments, where it feeds on amphibians, reptiles, fishes, and sometimes mammals. (138)

Red-bellied Water Snake
A two-toned water snake, also called the "copperbelly." Occasional flashes of its red lower belly contrast with its dark brown back. The back color may vary from gray to green. This southern snake can be found at some distance from water during hot, humid weather. (139)

Red-bellied Snake

Unrelated to the Red-bellied Water Snake, this species is usually light brown with a lighter brown stripe along the back and pale markings on the head. The bright red belly is yellow in some individuals. This small snake hunts earthworms, insects, and other arthropods. It is abundant at higher elevations in the Northeast, and lives in open woods. (140)

Eastern Garter Snake

This subspecies of the Common Garter Snake is widely distributed and highly variable in color and pattern. It has a pale stripe down the middle of the back and light side stripes. These stripes contrast with a darker, often checked, band along the side. Below these markings, the ground color may be the same as the stripe or a darker color. Some individuals may have yellow, brown, green, or bluish stripes. The ground color may be black, dark brown, green, or olive. This commonly seen snake thrives in a wide variety of habitats, such as marshes, pastures, and drainage ditches. You may also meet it in city parks and cemeteries. (141)

Western Ribbon Snake

A long, slender snake with a bright orange, yellow, or brownish stripe down the middle of the back, and a pale stripe low on each side. The color on the sides between stripes is brown, gray, or black. The belly is light yellow. This snake is a good swimmer. It stays close to water and eats small fishes and tadpoles. (142)

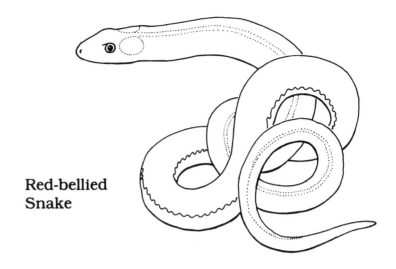

Red-bellied
Snake

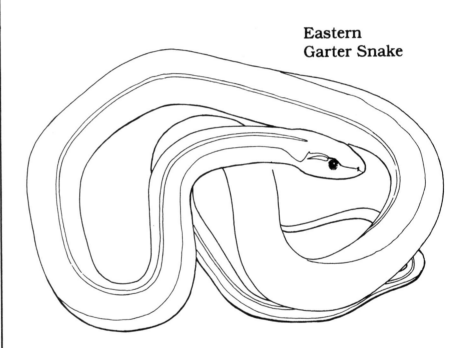

Eastern
Garter Snake

Western
Ribbon Snake

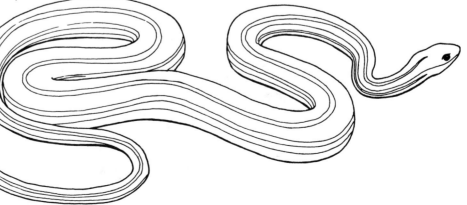

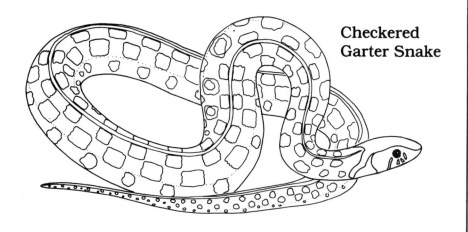

**Checkered
Garter Snake**

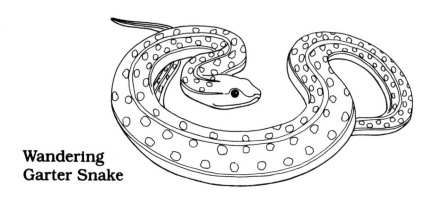

**Wandering
Garter Snake**

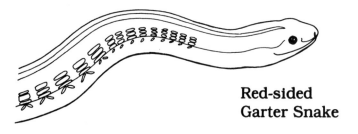

**Red-sided
Garter Snake**

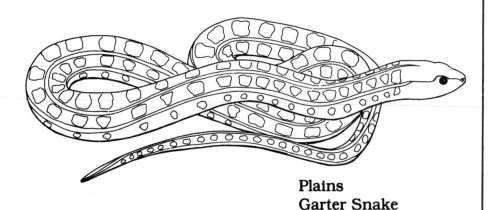

**Plains
Garter Snake**

Checkered Garter Snake
Distinct black spots on olive or
light brown form a checker-
board pattern. The snake has a
narrow, orange or yellow stripe
down the back. A light crescent
is backed by black on each side
behind the head. Found
throughout the arid Southwest,
this snake is rarely far from
water. Nocturnal in the southern part of its range, it becomes active during the day in
cooler northern areas. It hunts
small prey in streams and irri-
gation ditches. (143)

Wandering Garter Snake
Like most other garter snakes,
this one varies in color. Choose
brown, greenish brown, buff, or
gray for the background. The
pale side stripe is light yellow.
Most individuals have a pale,
dull yellow or brown stripe
down the back and darker
spots. Found in a variety of
habitats, this garter snake frequents open grasslands and
forests, but is usually near
water. It is a subspecies of the
Western Terrestrial Garter
Snake. (144)

Red-sided Garter Snake
This is a subspecies of the
Common Garter Snake. Dark
spots and red bars mark the
sides. The stripes are usually
broad and dull. The head is
dark olive above and light below. Like other garter snakes,
this animal produces a foul-
smelling substance when
caught. (145)

Plains Garter Snake
This garter snake may not be
as easy to identify as it is fun
to color. Its colors vary, and
some individuals may be so
dark that the markings are ob-
scured. A bright yellow or orange stripe runs down the
middle of the back. Below this
stripe are rows of black spots
on an olive to reddish brown
background. A pale yellow
stripe set low on each side is
bordered below by a row of dark
dots on olive-brown. (146)

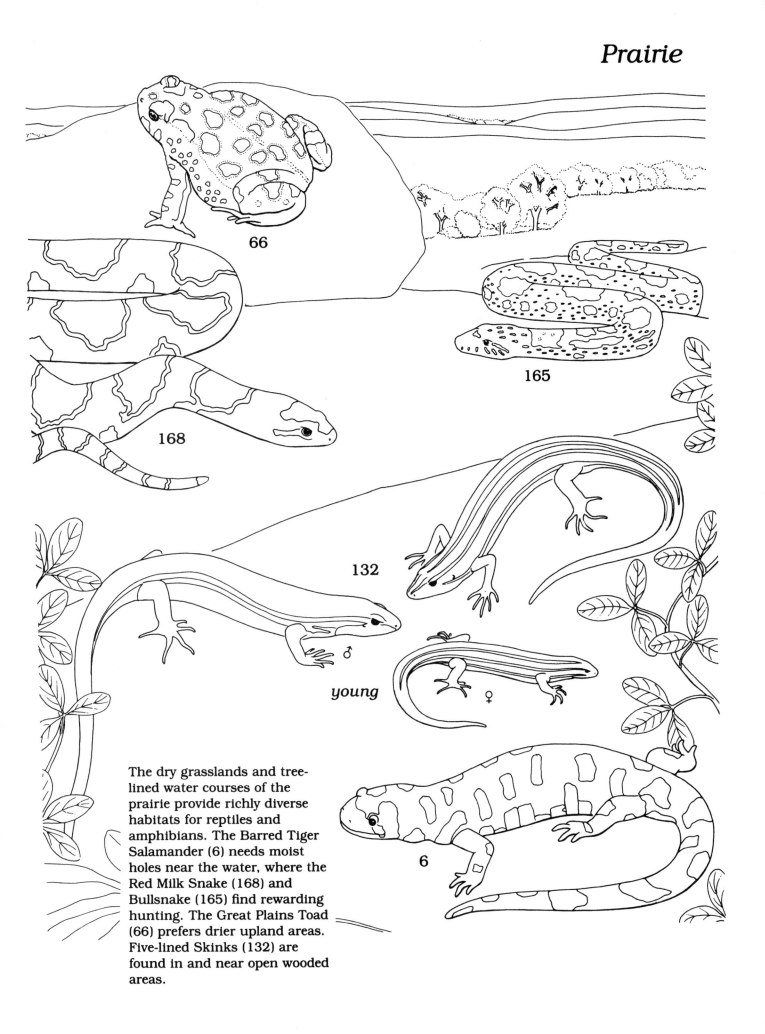

66

165

168

132

young

The dry grasslands and tree-lined water courses of the prairie provide richly diverse habitats for reptiles and amphibians. The Barred Tiger Salamander (6) needs moist holes near the water, where the Red Milk Snake (168) and Bullsnake (165) find rewarding hunting. The Great Plains Toad (66) prefers drier upland areas. Five-lined Skinks (132) are found in and near open wooded areas.

6

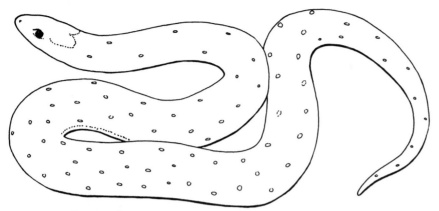

**Smooth
Earth Snake**

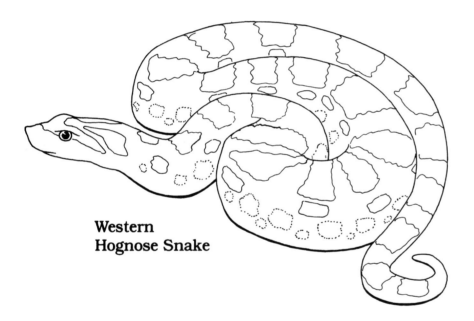

**Western
Hognose Snake**

Smooth Earth Snake
Small black flecks are widely spaced on a brown or gray ground color. The belly is light. Limited to the eastern United States, this secretive snake prefers abandoned fields near forests. It may be found burrowing in loose soil and leaf litter for earthworms, slugs, and insects. It hiberates under rocks and in soil. (147)

Western Hognose Snake
You can identify this thick-bodied snake by its upturned snout. The belly has black markings. A mixture of dark and light brown spots show against the tan or gray back. The head has large brown marks. When frightened, hognose snakes roll over on their back and, after a few jerks, lie still as though dead. This western species hunts lizards and amphibians in its dry prairie habitat. (148)

Eastern Hognose Snake
The colors vary in this hognose snake, but it generally has large black blotches on a mixed yellow and brown background. It plays dead more often than its western counterpart, and is more apt to inflate itself first by spreading its neck and head and gulping air. It also hisses loudly. This display makes the snake seem dangerous, even though it is harmless. (149)

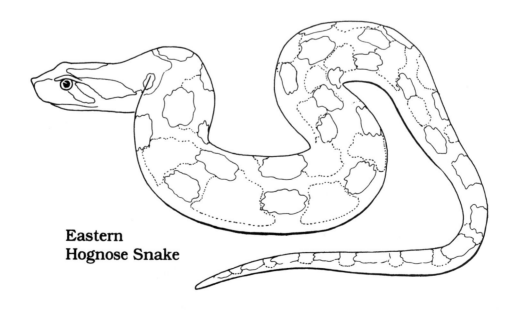

**Eastern
Hognose Snake**

Ringneck Snake

A slender, unmarked snake with a light yellow or orange ring around its neck. The belly is bright yellow or orange. The tail has a bright red or yellow underside. When they are threatened, some ringneck snakes twist themselves into a coil and raise the tail to reveal its bright coloring. Active both day and night, this snake seeks protection under logs and damp rocks during the day. It eats woodland salamanders, small frogs and reptiles, insects, and earthworms. (150)

Sharp-tailed Snake

This snake is named for its sharp tail tip. An indistinct, light red or yellow line along each side interrupts the plain red or gray ground color. Although secretive, this snake can be found under objects after rain on warm days in the spring. Pastures near woodland at low elevations are good places to look for this snake. It feeds on slugs. (151)

Mud Snake

A large, shiny, black or dark gray snake. The red belly marks extend onto its sides. The lower jaw is light yellow with black spots. This southern snake frequents swamps and ponds where it hunts for salamanders. It may use its stiff tail to jab its prey while maneuvering it into a good position for swallowing. The tail is also used against human captors, giving rise to the name "horn snake." (152)

Rainbow Snake

This glossy reptile has red stripes on a black background. The belly is red with black spots, and the sides are striped with yellow and red. The upper head is mottled with red and black. The Rainbow Snake eats eels, which it catches in streams of cypress swamps. '153)

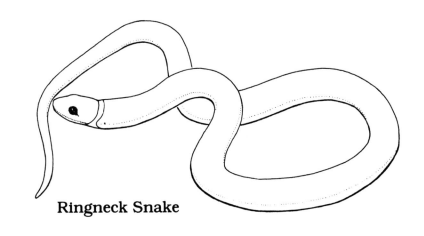

Ringneck Snake

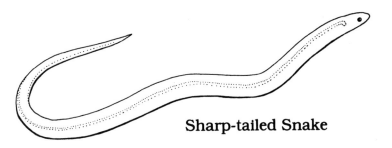

Sharp-tailed Snake

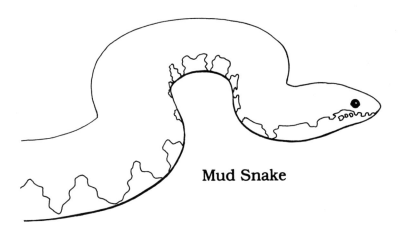

Mud Snake

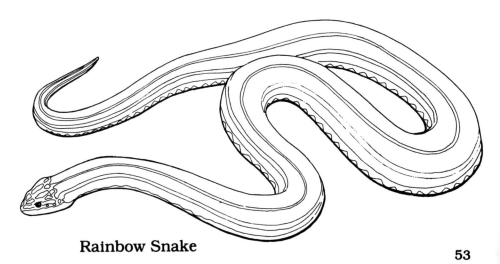

Rainbow Snake

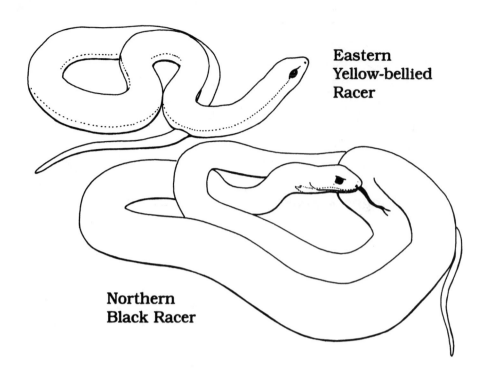

Eastern
Yellow-bellied
Racer

Northern
Black Racer

Eastern Coachwhip

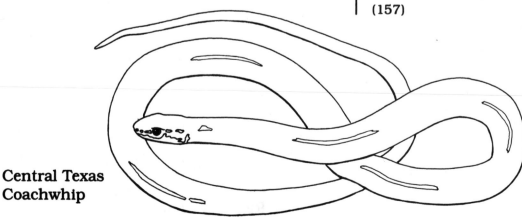

Central Texas
Coachwhip

Eastern Yellow-bellied Racer
A variable subspecies of the Racer. The brown, gray, olive, or dark blue back contrasts with the bright yellow belly. You may glimpse this snake as it moves rapidly through low vegetation. It hunts rodents, small birds, and insects in daylight. (154)

Northern Black Racer
This snake is also a subspecies of the Racer. Larger than its colorful relative, the Eastern Yellow-bellied Racer, this snake is uniformly dark with small white markings on its chin. (155)

Eastern Coachwhip
A southern species of the Coachwhip. The color changes from dark on the head to light on the tail. Some individuals have dark coloring only on the head; others may be dark only on the front half, or almost entirely dark. The long slender tail resembles a whip. When hunting in rugged terrain, this snake moves swiftly, often with its head held well above the ground. (156)

Central Texas Coachwhip
Another subspecies of the Coachwhip. This slender, black, or reddish brown snake has irregular white patches along its sides, which become fainter toward the tail. The underside of the tail is bright pink. This snake moves rapidly in the arid vegetation of dry valleys in central Texas. It prefers small mammals and lizards for food. (157)

Rough Green Snake

An agile, slender, brightly colored snake. It is green above and pale green or yellowish below. The dorsal scales have ridges (keels) running down their centers. These keeled scales give the snake a rough appearance. This snake hunts grasshoppers, caterpillars, and spiders in dense plant growth near streams. (158)

Great Plains Rat Snake

This is a subspecies of the Corn Snake. Dark gray or brown blotches edged in black contrast with the light gray background. These colors form a bold "V" on top of the head. Note the dark eyestripe. Nocturnal, especially during the summer, this snake hides by day in the numerous rock crevices of the dry creeks and valleys where it lives. (159)

Corn Snake

The Corn Snake's markings are similar to those of the Great Plains Rat Snake, but are more brightly colored. This attractive snake sports reddish blotches against a background of tan, gray, yellow, or orange. Often found in or near rodent burrows, it catches small mammals for food. Woodlots, barnyards, and abandoned houses in the Southeast are the preferred habitat of this snake. (160)

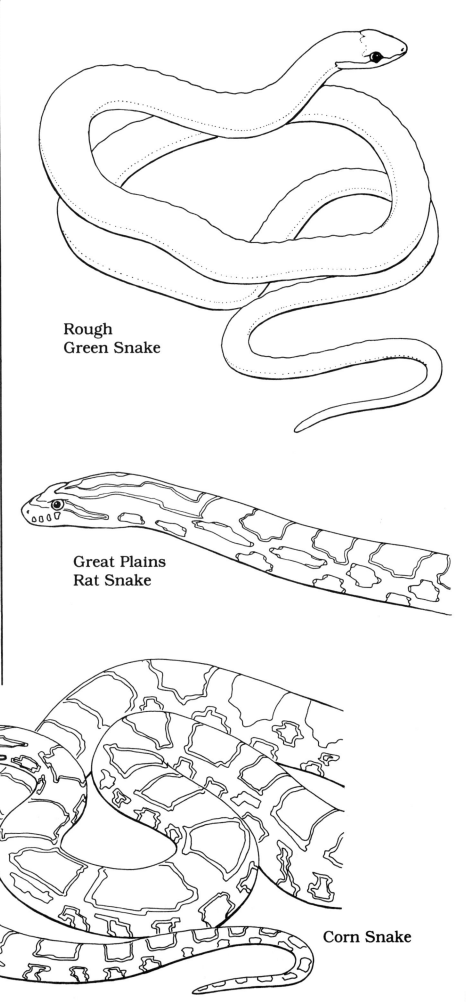

Rough
Green Snake

Great Plains
Rat Snake

Corn Snake

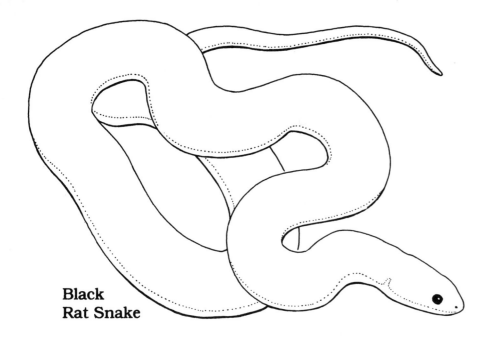

**Black
Rat Snake**

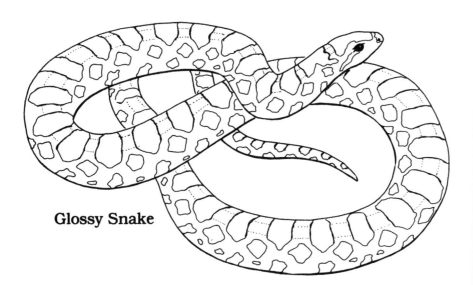

Glossy Snake

Black Rat Snake

This is a subspecies of the Rat Snake. The belly is pale, but the rest of the snake is shiny black. A faint pattern shows when the body is distended after a meal. This snake lives in a variety of habitats in the Northeast, from the coastal plain to the Appalachians. It hunts small mammals and birds, both on the ground and in trees, and constricts its prey. (161)

Glossy Snake

Give the markings on the Glossy Snake a faded appearance. They are light brown edged in black on a cream or buff background. A dark eyeline runs to the jaw. This snake is active during the evening and early morning. It feeds on lizards that are common in the arid Southwest. (162)

The next three snakes are all related.

Northern Pine Snake

A powerful, constricting snake that burrows after rodents. It lives mainly in flat, sandy pine barrens of the South and East. The ground color may be yellowish or light gray. Black, irregular blotches become browner toward the tail. This reptile is secretive and rarely seen. (163)

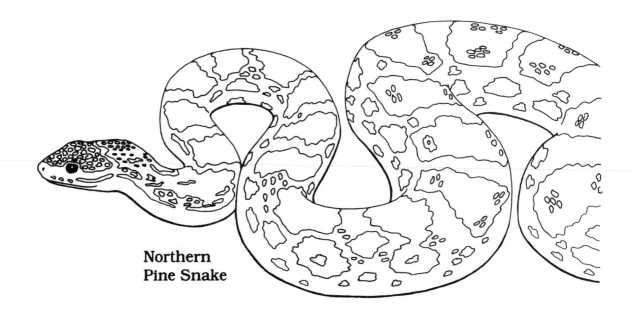

**Northern
Pine Snake**

Gopher Snake

In this large snake, the brown or reddish brown markings, speckled with black, contrast with a yellow or cream-colored background. A dark line runs between the eyes and down to the jaw. Gopher snakes are found in a wide variety of habitats throughout western North America. They eat rodents and occasionally lizards, killing their prey by constriction. (164)

Bullsnake

This animal also appears in the Prairie Scene, p. 51. Like gopher snakes, it has a dark line running from eye to jaw. Black or brown blotches against a cream background cover the entire body, with the strongest contrast at the head and tail. Smaller dots speckle the sides. The belly is yellow with bold black dots extending onto the lower sides. Dry plains and prairie with clumps of vegetation provide excellent hunting grounds for this snake. (165)

Eastern Kingsnake

A subspecies of the Common Kingsnake. White or cream-colored links between shiny black patches give this snake its folk name, the "chain snake." The animal is common in the pine woods of the East Coast. It hunts near water, in marshes, and along streams, where it feeds on water snakes and turtle eggs. In spring and autumn, watch for this snake out hunting at dawn or dusk. You may see it basking on mats of streamside plants. (166)

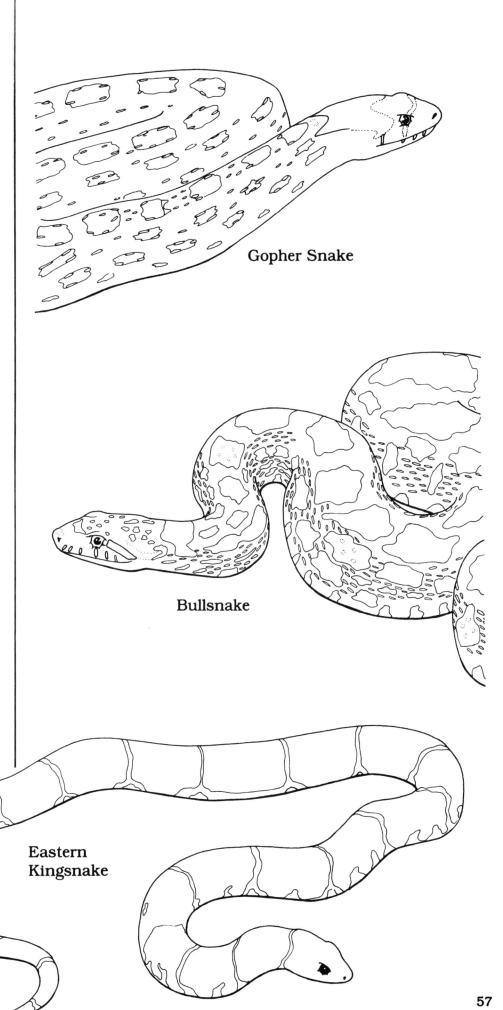

Gopher Snake

Bullsnake

Eastern Kingsnake

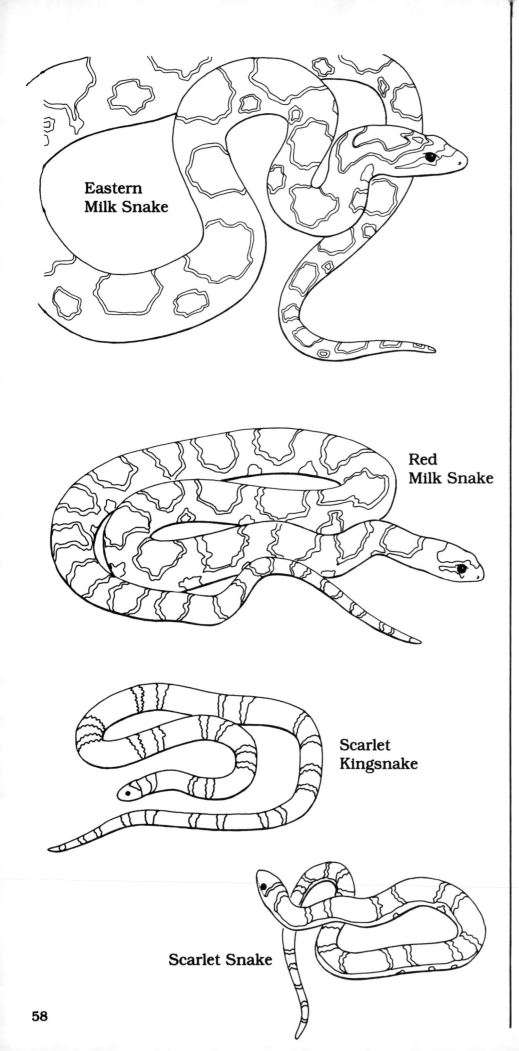

Eastern Milk Snake

Red Milk Snake

Scarlet Kingsnake

Scarlet Snake

Eastern Milk Snake
Large, black-edged, red or brown blotches on the back alternate with similar but smaller marks on the sides. The background is white, light cream, or gray. The marking at the back of the head may be Y- or V-shaped. Since it hunts mice in barns, the Milk Snake has been falsely accused of milking cows, which is how it got its name. This subspecies lives in many habitats, including woodlands, rocky hillsides, and fields. (167)

Red Milk Snake
Also shown in the Prairie Scene, p. 51. This subspecies has a light collar and smaller markings along the sides. The dorsal blotches extend further down onto the sides than in the Eastern Milk Snake. (168)

Scarlet Kingsnake
Another subspecies of the Milk Snake. This brightly colored subspecies has a color pattern that mimics that of the venomous Coral Snake (p. 60). Although this snake is nonpoisonous, the warning coloration helps protect it from predators. The red snout and black rings, which separate yellow rings from wide red bands, distinguish the Scarlet Kingsnake. It lives in pine woodlands, hiding during the day in logs and under bark (see Eastern Woodlands Scene, p. 27). Heavy rains may bring it out. It feeds on small snakes and earthworms. (169)

Scarlet Snake
This colorful, nonpoisonous snake is another mimic of the Coral Snake. You can recognize this snake by its red snout and the different sequence of band colors. Broad red patches alternate with narrow yellow areas. Black bands separate these two colors. The belly is white. The Scarlet Snake preys on young lizards and mice, which it kills by constriction. It also eats eggs, crushing the larger ones and swallowing the smaller ones. (170)

Texas Long-nosed Snake
A subspecies of the Long-nosed Snake. Red and black bands separated by yellow extend the entire length of this snake. The red bands are speckled with black, and the black bands are speckled with yellow. The head is mostly black. Young are paler in color than adults. This snake rests during the day under desert rocks or in dry prairie burrows and hunts at night for lizards, eggs, and rodents. (171)

Ground Snake
A secretive snake of the arid Southwest and Mexico. This species varies greatly in color and pattern. Sometimes two very different-looking individuals (one banded or striped, one plain) can be found under the same rock. Three forms are shown here for you to color. The first Ground Snake has dark crossbands only on the neck; color the rest of it reddish above, and paler red below (172). Color the next form light brown above and yellow below (173). In the third Ground Snake (174), dark crossbands form broad black saddles across the back. The area between the black blotches or saddles can be orange.

Sonoran Shovel-nosed Snake
A snake of Arizona's upland desert, where it occupies coarse rocky areas with mesquite and cactus. A good burrower. Strong black crossbands alternate with broad red bands on a whitish yellow background. A black band surrounds the eye. The convex snout is yellow. (175)

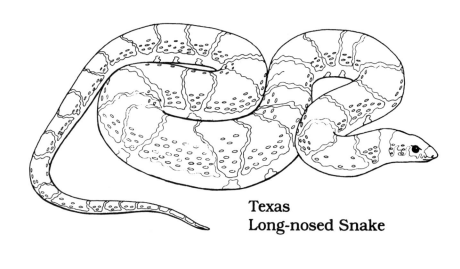

Texas
Long-nosed Snake

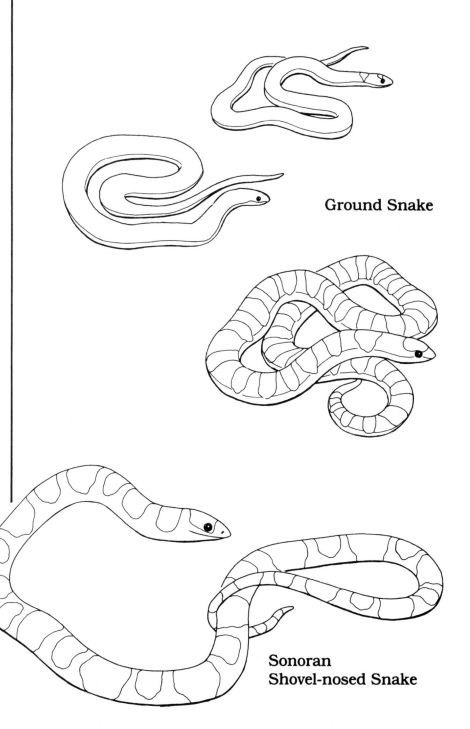

Ground Snake

Sonoran
Shovel-nosed Snake

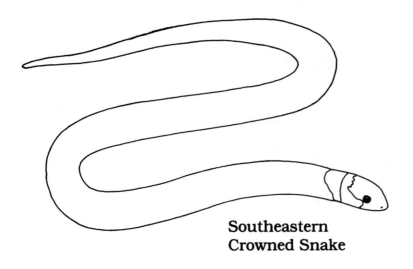

Southeastern Crowned Snake

Western Coral Snake

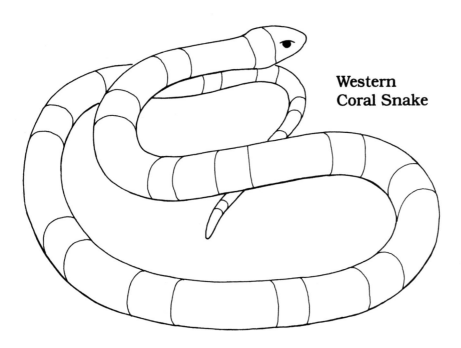

Southeastern Crowned Snake
A small, reddish brown snake. It has a black head with a light band across the rear part. Look for this secretive snake under logs in swamps, dry woods, or backyards in the Southeast. It eats centipedes and insect larvae. (176)

Western Coral Snake
The brilliant colors of the Western Coral Snake warn potential predators that it is poisonous. Broad, alternating bands of black and red encircle the body. They are separated by yellow or white. The head is black. This snake lives in the arid Southwest in various habitats, but is most abundant in rocky upland desert with loose soil and rocks. It hides its head in body coils when disturbed, showing the tail tip above the coils. (177)

Eastern Coral Snake
A highly poisonous snake that is red, yellow, and black. You can tell it from harmless mimics by its black snout and yellow head band. The body is shiny. Broad, black and red bands speckled with black are separated by yellow. These snakes are active by day in both dry and moist environments. (178)

Eastern Coral Snake

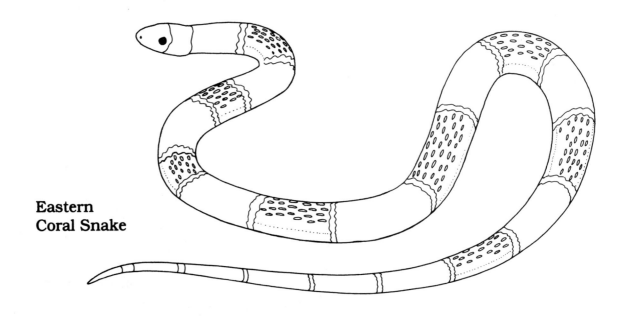

Northern Copperhead

A reddish body camouflages this venomous snake against leaf litter in eastern deciduous woodlands. The head is coppery red. Dark brown bands are broad at the sides and narrow on the back. This snake hunts mice and frogs and normally is not very aggressive, but it will strike if cornered. It hibernates in groups, often with other species of snakes. (179)

Eastern Cottonmouth

Also shown in the Southern Swamp Scene, p. 37. Always associated with water, this large-bodied snake is highly poisonous. When aroused, it shows the white inside of its mouth. The body color varies from olive to brown or black above, with a light belly. The crossbands have distinct borders and are lighter in their centers. The pattern is less distinct in older individuals. These snakes are difficult to distinguish from harmless water snakes. In the South, all water snakes should be watched with care. (180)

Massasauga

The Massasauga has large, dark spots circled with lighter color along its dark gray back. Rows of smaller spots dot the sides. Like other rattlesnakes, the Massasauga has a tail that ends in a rattle. New segments are added to the rattle each time the snake sheds its skin, but since this may occur more than once a year or not at all, the number of segments do not tell a rattlesnake's age. The Massasauga lives in wet habitats in the eastern United States and may hide in crayfish holes. It hunts mice and other small rodents in swamps. (181)

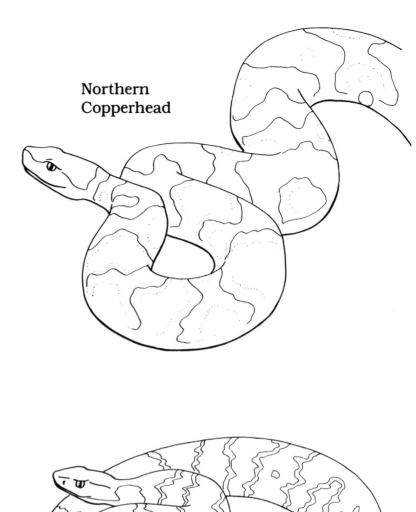

Northern
Copperhead

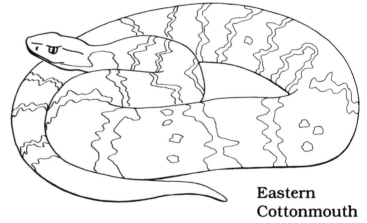

Eastern
Cottonmouth

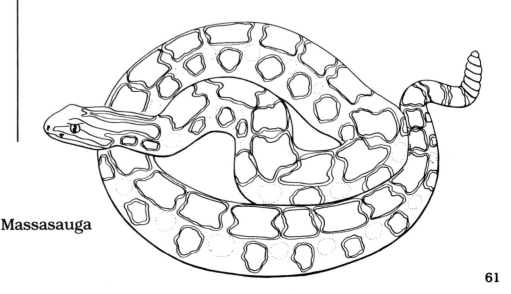

Massasauga

61

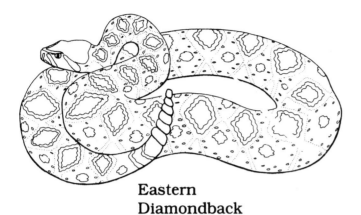

Eastern
Diamondback
Rattlesnake

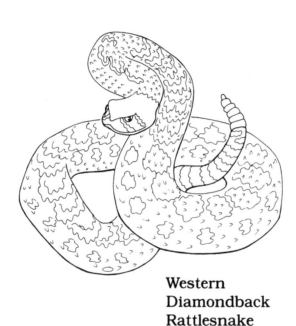

Western
Diamondback
Rattlesnake

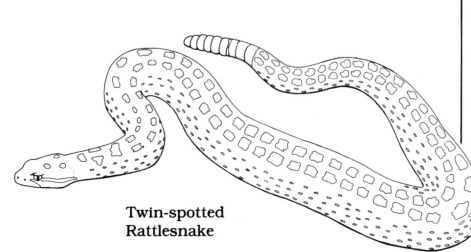

Twin-spotted
Rattlesnake

Eastern Diamondback Rattlesnake

Avoid close contact with this very dangerous snake, except while coloring this drawing. The diamond-shaped markings on the back are dark brown. They are surrounded by cream-colored scales against a background of olive, brown, or black. The pattern is less bright in individuals preparing to shed their skin. The head has two light lines near each eye and vertical lines on the snout. The bite of this snake is fatal to rats, and often to people. It lives in many habitats in the Southeast. (182)

Western Diamondback Rattlesnake

A large, intimidating snake with a loud rattle. The diamond-shaped markings are often not clearly defined. General colors are brown or gray, occasionally with red or yellow tinges. The tail is ringed with black and white, hence the folk name "coontail rattler." Individuals will sometimes raise their heads high above the body coils when preparing to strike at an enemy. This rattlesnake is found in the arid Southwest, where it feeds on small mammals, lizards, and occasionally birds. (183)

Twin-spotted Rattlesnake

Two rows of small, dark brown spots extend the length of this snake. Smaller spots dot the sides. A dark line extending from the eye is underlined with white. The snake is usually gray-brown with brown tail bands. It lives in rocky, high mountain areas with mixed woodlands and forest. Like all rattlesnakes, it has heat-sensitive pits on its upper snout that help it hunt small mammals. It also eats lizards. (184)

Mojave Rattlesnake

This rattlesnake's diamond-shaped marks are clearly outlined in light yellow. The background is often greenish gray. Light stripes extend from the eye to the corner of the mouth. The tail has narrow dark bands on a whitish background. This snake likes open desert with sparse vegetation. As in all rattlesnake species, the female gives birth to live young. (185)

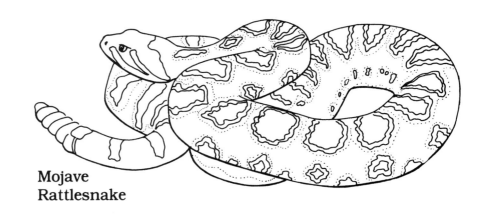

Mojave
Rattlesnake

Ridge-nosed Rattlesnake

A mountain snake of mixed pine forests and woodland, the Ridge-nosed Rattlesnake is sometimes seen basking on sunny slopes. Look for the white crossbars edged with black or brown on its reddish brown back. The snout has a ridge from above the eye to the nostril. The sides of the head are brown or reddish brown, marked with white lines. (186)

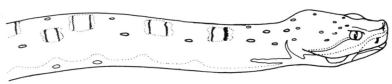

Ridge-nosed
Rattlesnake

Sidewinder

Also shown in the Desert Scene, p. 64. A small rattlesnake. Its rapid sideways movement lets it crawl very quickly and limits the amount of belly in contact with the hot desert sand. It has a projecting scale above each eye. The pale yellow or tan coloring and inconspicuous pattern blend with the snake's sandy environment. The Sidewinder adds to this camouflage by partly burying itself in the sand. (187)

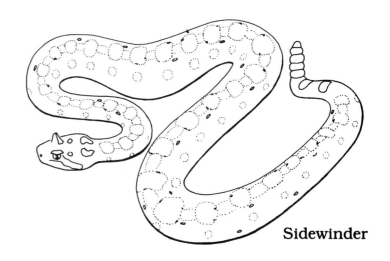

Sidewinder

Canebrake Rattlesnake

The Canebrake is a subspecies of the Timber Rattlesnake. Dark V-shaped patches mark the pale gray or brown back. The markings become less conspicuous toward the tail, where the ground color becomes darker. A reddish brown stripe runs down the back, and a dark stripe lies behind the eye. This snake frequents swamplands and thickets in the Southeast. (188)

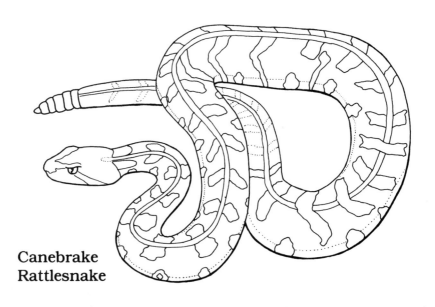

Canebrake
Rattlesnake

Southwestern Desert

With their water-retaining skins, many reptiles are ideally suited to deserts. All have ways of adapting their behavior to control their body heat. The Desert Tortoise (93) retreats to the shade during the heat of the day. The Chuckwalla (97) and Side-blotched Lizard (107) bask in the sun to raise their body temperatures. The Sidewinder (187), when it occasionally ventures out by day, avoids contact with the hot sand through its sideways movement.

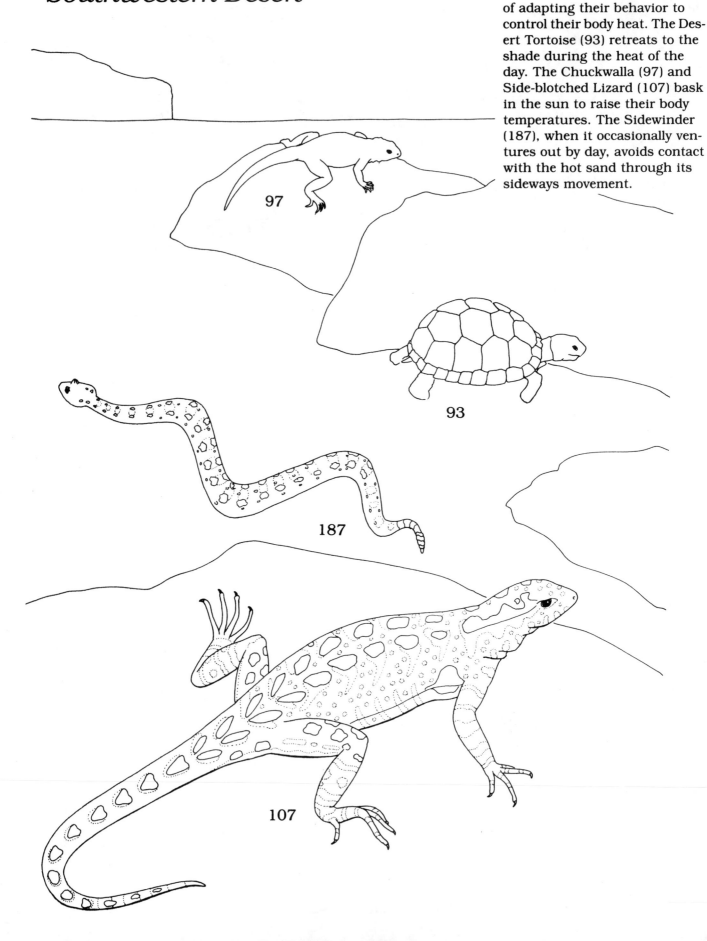